MAX WEBER AND VALUE-FREE SOCIOLOGY

SOCIOLOGY

A Marxist Critique

MAX WEBER AND
VALUE-FREE SOCIOLOGY

A Marxist Critique

by

John Lewis

1975
LAWRENCE AND WISHART
LONDON

1

Copyright © John Lewis 1975

ISBN 0 85315 339 6 hardback
ISBN 0 85315 340 x paperback

Printed in Great Britain by
The Camelot Press Ltd, Southampton

Contents

The whole understanding of the facts is halted where the scientific scholar permits the intrusion of his own value judgments.

Weber, *Wissenschaft als Beruf*

Whoever lacks the capacity to put on blinkers may as well stay away from science. Without this you have no calling for science and you should be doing something else.

Weber, *Essays in Sociology*

Preface

Max Weber may not be very widely read in Britain today, but his ideas retain their currency. He remains a figure of the first importance in sociology. For he was the first non-Marxist to see that a sociology based on a simple description of social data and deriving its generalisations from such data, endeavouring to follow the methods of the natural sciences, was logically unsound and inadequate as a method for the social sciences. It does no more than describe and analyse present society without considering its fundamental structure and economic basis as themselves problematic.

Weber attempted to provide a philosophical understanding of capitalist society that went beyond the mindless empiricism that eschewed theory in favour of a practical concern with plain facts. He wanted to show that capitalism was not merely a contingent fact of history and might as well have been something quite different, but that it was the inevitable consequence of a principle of rationalisation which he saw as having increasingly pervaded and dominated the Western world from the birth of science in the seventeenth century. Weber attempted to show how on this basis a rational economy and its necessary system of social relations came into existence. In the second place, he demonstrated the necessity of a system of bureaucratic control and government authority to sustain and organise such a system, and how its legitimacy came to be accepted and was supported thanks to the charisma of the ruling élite.

Thirdly, he sought to prove that such a system must exclude interference with its working on moral grounds, in terms of human rights, natural justice or public welfare. His sociology is therefore value-free in both its treatment of the economy and of the social order in general.

Weber's sociology, with its philosophical justification, proved more satisfactory as a rationale for capitalism than conventional empiricism. One reason for this was the increasing appearance of disequilibrium, anomalies, irrationalities and social conflict—facts which did not validate the claims of capitalism to a justification of the same kind as that of scientific systems in the natural order. The stars in their courses do not present us with an increasing disparity between fact and theory such as has become indisputable in the study of capitalism. These facts did not disturb Weber. From the first he was aware of the 'substantive irrationalities' which resulted from the working of the rational laws of society. Moreover, he never claimed that his theory of capitalism was empirically derived and dependent upon social fact. It was advanced as no more than a pragmatic model or 'ideal type' whose usefulness outweighed its incompatibility with a good many of the facts it sought to explain.

Weber's sociology, by substituting the notion of 'ideal types' and laws strictly inferred from specific cultures and by no means universal, was constructed on quite a different model from the theories of the natural sciences. It has, in fact, been far more satisfactory as a method than the attempt to use the ordinary methods of the natural sciences in the study of society.

But when the credentials of Weber's more sophisticated

sociology are examined it at once reveals one striking feature, its lack of the historical dimension. Nor is its pragmatic epistemology philosophically satisfactory. Its claim to go beyond empiricism cannot be substantiated either. It does not really attempt to do more than find a pragmatic justification for things as they are.

What emerges from this critique is the need for a more genuinely scientific sociology, with a satisfactory philosophical basis, based on the sequence of economic and social forms arising in human history, and the corresponding types of civilisation that constitute the story of mankind.

Max Weber, Man and Fighter

The work of Max Weber is unquestionably one of the outstanding contributions to the making of sociology. As a thinker he was steeped in the tradition of Kant and deeply involved in the economic and political problems raised by Karl Marx. His philosophical position derived directly from his close association with the Heidelberg group of neo-Kantian philosophers, especially Rickert.[1] He accepted their distinction between the natural sciences and historical and social questions. It was from this point of view that he carried out his investigations into the origin and nature of capitalism and developed his concept of a value-free science of society.

He died in 1920 at the early age of fifty-six, leaving behind him not only his major theoretical works, but a great mass of technical studies in various fields, much of it uncompleted. With his encyclopaedic mind he was indeed a scholar of immense erudition, carrying out comparative studies in social and cultural phenomena throughout past history, including exhaustive inquiries into Roman antiquity and the economics of slave labour. Particularly important were his discussions on the legitimacy of government, bureaucracy and the charisma of leadership.

He even turned from political theory to the sociology of the arts and wrote a treatise on *The Rational and Social Foundations of Music* containing an interesting chapter on 'The Emergence of the Piano as a Modern Keyboard Instrument'. His early death meant that he left many unfinished works and plans for further books. His students' lecture notes survive, but not the lectures themselves.

Among his major works, the *General Economic History* is perhaps the most readable for those wanting an introduction to his position, and his *Theory of Social and Economic Organisation*, in which he develops his view of the nature of capitalist society. In 1905, *The Protestant Ethic and the Spirit of Capitalism* appeared, perhaps his best known book, in which he advanced the theory that the essence of capitalism was to be found not in its economic system but in the changed ideology of Western Europe which resulted in the Protestant Reformation.

The basis of his treatment of capitalist society was undoubtedly Marx's *Capital*. But whereas Marx saw in it the progressive emergence of contradictions in its structure which pointed to its transformation, for Weber it represented a completed institutionalised system, oriented to making profits and to the acquisitive exploitation of the market system. Rickert had convinced him that it could not be studied in the manner of the physical sciences, and the method that Weber proposed was strikingly original. It was to construct what he called an 'ideal type' of capitalism, to be regarded, however, not as a hypothesis or theory derived from an empirical study of the existing data, but rather as a suggestion that in capitalist society things happened *as if* they followed his model. His 'ideal type' might be taken not so much as an empirical theory as a *useful fiction* in a pragmatic sense.

In addition to his academic work Weber was deeply concerned with German politics and was frequently urged to enter completely into political activities. His commanding personality and great gifts as a speaker, his courage and evident integrity, would have served him well had he done so; but until the revolution of 1918 he drew back. He then intervened to support the combination of the Right-wing Social Democrats and the Army to crush the communist uprising, and afterwards gave his advice in the drawing up of the Weimar Constitution.

His whole philosophy had an overt political intention. It was first and foremost based on his conviction of "the primary interests of the nation state"; this involved forthright criticism of the policies of the Kaiser and the autocratic Bismarckian Constitution. He represented the nationalist convictions of the leading business interests who called themselves Liberals, and meant by that the enchancement of the business interests of the German State. He was well aware that the influence of Marx was greater in Germany, where the Social Democractic Party was a power to be reckoned with, than in any other country. And both politically and in his theoretical work his career could be considered a long epic campaign against the power of Marxism.

This might give the impression of Weber as an out-and-out reactionary. This was by no means the case. German capitalism, for years far behind that of Britain and France, was a progressive force at that time and there was a good deal of aristocratic lumber and religious conservatism hampering its development, as there had been in Britain fifty years before. He was a man of profound convictions, formidable knowledge and penetrating understanding of the sociology and politics of a still advancing capitalism. But he had no illusions about its principles, or what it meant for human values. They were to be swept ruthlessly aside if in any way they hampered the functioning of his value-free economy. Unlike the more sentimental defenders of capitalism he never pretended that it was in every way 'a good thing'. It was necessary for the welfare of the German State, and this was the one value that mattered. The price that mankind had to pay he knew to be a heavy one. He spoke of 'the disenchanted world' for which capitalism was responsible. He agreed with Simmel and Tönnies that from the standpoint of humanity the capitalist scene was a hateful one and he despaired of its consequences.

Weber was a typical member of his class. On the one side, both he and his wife came from leading industrial families, and enjoyed the moderate wealth that gave him security and the possibilities of leisure and travel. On the other, he had relatives and friends in the academic world who made his place in the realms of scholarship one of importance in the many universities where he was always welcome. This gave him also the indulgence he so generously received for long absences for travel and rest and above all from what he called "the torture of teaching". Nevertheless he spent some twenty years at Heidelberg and held other professorships too, and gathered around him devoted colleagues and disciples, many of whom still remember him.

He was one of the founders of the German Sociological Association and gathered his friends together at the regular meetings on Sunday afternoons of what came to be known as the Max Weber Circle—among them Troeltsch, Jellinek, Jaspers and Lukács. After his death his wife, Marianne Weber, revived the tradition; and it has continued to the present day.

There were three intellectual and spiritual forces which played an important part in the making of his mind: Rickert, Dilthey and Simmel set his mind on the track of a science of culture which could grasp those historical realities that slipped through the meshes of the physical sciences. His family was in the religious tradition of a vigorous German Protestantism, and in its piety and ethical principles he discerned one of the creative impulses of capitalism. Paradoxically he found an equally powerful influence in the philosophy of Nietzsche, from whom he derived his belief in élitism and the authority of a master class on the one hand, and on the other his contempt for a slave morality and the worthless humanitarianism that stood in the way of the spirit of capitalism and German nationalism. He believed in the worth of nothing but the purposeful thought and behaviour which mercilessly establish and apply the means necessary for economic and political self-assertion.

Reason of state was the reason above all other and lesser reasons. We catch the passion and urgency of his conviction, and the loyalty of his masterful spirit and ascetic dedicated calling, in the very accents of his speech and writing which could often be harsh and strident, full of phrases which reveal his militant nationalism and his contempt for what he saw as maudlin sentimentality. The core of his philosophy was the view that social life was essentially "a struggle of man against man". His creed was the first unambiguous appearance of Social Darwinism as a political philosophy. He demanded that no one should deceive himself as to the fundamental fact that social existence and national culture depend on power—a necessity that would never diminish.

It is not peace and happiness that we shall hand over to our descendants, but rather the principle of eternal struggle for the survival of the superior creed of our national species.[2]

We should recognise that Weber's gloomy recognition of the harshness of the operation of capitalist economic laws did not so much reflect callousness to human suffering as a realistic appreciation of the inevitability of alienation and suffering under capitalism—a fact which actually brought him nearer to Marxism than the complacent belief in the universal beneficence of the capitalist economy. So also his imperialism was not mere chauvinist aggrandisement but the recognition that imperialist policies had become necessary for the survival of the capitalist State at this stage of its economic development. This understanding of economic imperialism was reached in the same period, that leading up to 1914, by Hilferding in Austria, Kautsky and Rosa Luxemburg in Germany, and J. A. Hobson in Britain. Lenin expressed his indebtedness to Hobson in his own important work *Imperialism, the Highest Stage of Capitalism* (1917); and in Varga's new edition the work of Kautsky and Hilferding was also recognised.

The argument was that in the stage of finance capitalism the export of capital on an increasing scale was imperative if the system were not to collapse. This was recognised by Weber, who declared that in view of the military strength of Britain and France, even at the risk of war, Germany must become their equal in power; secondly, she must annex whatever strips of territory were essential for her strategic safety; and finally she must create an east-central European *cordon sanitaire* of autonomous Slav nation-states under German hegemony as a bulwark against Russia.[3] This was an extraordinarily perceptive judgement of the economic necessity of imperialist policies.

A lasting merit of Max Weber is that he was the first to demonstrate the premises of socio-economic dynamics on the basis of an analysis of the nature and development of capitalism. He saw the necessity for certain modes of action and political decision which took place for the first time in the years leading up to the first world war. As a consequence he was furious against the pacifist tendencies of the Left-wing German socialist movement during and after the war, which in the post-war period was endangering her position. He envisaged a post-war political order in Europe and the world at large in which Great Power policies would control the world.

He was quite candid about the undeniable fact that it was the ruling class which always gained most from successful imperialist operations. His political policy therefore was not only concerned with Germany's survival as a nation-state, but became a manipulative strategy of a ruling élite designed to defend its privileged position. Linking this economic situation with the danger threatened by the rise of the Social Democratic Party, it was aimed at forestalling the imminent rise of the working class to power.

Every successful policy of coercing other countries as a rule—or at any rate initially—also strengthens the domestic prestige and thereby the power and influence of those classes, status groups and parties under whose leadership success has been attained.[4]

We see that the ideology, the economics and the politics are three manifestations of a remarkable personality whose influence, far beyond Germany, extends particularly into the whole of the English-speaking world. We have here a man whose importance for the thinking of this generation cannot be limited to his views on sociology or a value-free science of man. His concept of power was oriented to the passionate, elemental determination to face up to the problems of the master race and the master class in the framework of the European struggle, external and internal, for domination. This concerns the two spheres—that of internal politics, the war against Marxism; and that of external politics, the war against England and France.

His direction in both internal and external politics, and likewise in his defence and exposition of capitalism, was always towards disenchantment and against the delusion of humanitarianism, towards awareness and the rational. Thanks to this realism he could free himself from traditions which for thousands of years have presented the world to man as a rational order informed by absolute values. What he developed in its place was an ideology of bitter disillusionment, of which he was acutely concious, sustained not unfittingly by an heroic faith, whose greatness and force have won admiration even from those who totally reject his philosophy.

NOTES

1. Brief information about authors quoted or mentioned will be found listed at the end of the book.
2. Weber, *Gesammelte Politischen Schriften*
3. Ibid.
4. Weber, *Wirtschaft und Gesellschaft*, vol. 2.

2

Durkheim and the Group Mind

The rending of the veil of the obvious which empiricism interposes between understanding and reality was the work primarily of Durkheim. But that was only a beginning; Durkheim was the first of a succession of thinkers who went beyond the straightforward facts of society to ask more fundamental questions. He was followed by Radcliffe-Brown, Weber, Talcott Parsons and others, who, together with the Neo-Kantian philosophers of the Heidelberg School, represented a major movement in the intellectual history of our time.

It is necessary to distinguish several phases in this development covering the space of some fifty years. The first was the phase of 'structural-functional' theory, which effectively shifted the emphasis from the model based on economics and physics to that of biology and anthropology. It was essentially organismic. Basic to this insight was the work of the French sociologist and anthropologist Emile Durkheim (1858–1917).

In his *Elementary Forms of the Religious Life*[1] Durkheim made clear the relevance of an integrated socio-cultural system to the understanding of society. He went far beyond the mere aggregation of individuals and groups or their atomic interaction. What became clear to him when investigating primitive cultures was that a society can only be understood if it is seen as a growing concern, as a moving whole which, like a spinning top, ceases to be itself if it ceases to be a *process* and becomes only a thing. Each culture is a distinctive living organism made up of inter-related parts, both sub-groups and individuals; and every such system must be seen as *in action*, pursuing corporate goals through purposeful operations. Institutions thus have to be seen as systems of meanings; and until the meaning behind it and its equally purposeful elements is grasped one does not see society at all. Anthropologists who now engage in long periods of field work tell us that only by living on intimate terms with a community for several years can one come to understand what people are up to, what their society really is. The anthropologist has to investigate, first, causal sequences or habitual behaviours; then the ends they serve and the part they play in a pre-figured complex of interlocking institutions. Gradually the meaning of this complex appears.

Sociologists took different views as to the over-riding goal of such societies. Malinowski saw it entirely in terms of survival. The notion of equilibrium (deriving powerful support from Cannon's physiological theories of *homeostasis*) became a matter of prime importance to Talcott Parsons, and eventually contemporary sociology came to see the determining principle of society as the maintenance of 'a steady state'.

We are looking at society in terms of an 'action frame' of reference—the term is Talcott Parsons'—but it is also, as Durkheim and Weber made clear, a system of beliefs and values. This may express itself in other cultures than our own in myths and symbols which may seem to us either fanciful or even ridiculous. Durkheim sees them as representing powerful emotional feelings of tribal unity and loyalty, of commitment and discipline, essential for maintaining unity and cohesion, forms related to kinship institutions and economic relations. In every society people share certain notions about their obligations and institutions and the form they should take; they know how rulers should treat their subjects, how subjects should behave to rulers, fathers to sons, tribesmen to chiefs. The categories of institutionalised social relationships are not fully intelligible unless the expectations and values underlying all the various roles men play in social life have been understood. It is the business of the sociologist to find this out.

If anyone imagines that all this is very far from what modern sociology is all about, it might be revealing to read Talcott Parsons' *Structure of Social Action* which shows how social stability and, indeed, the normal functioning of every society is maintained by a consensus acceptance of mutually coherent and balancing roles and expectations. It is this that Durkheim is feeling after. He was concerned with primitive societies which are easier to understand than our own, because their economy is simpler and the whole community can be examined in all its parts. But what is thus discovered about a simple 'native' community gives us the clue for understanding society as such, and our own community. We see at once that primitive societies are not all the same: the Azande of the Southern Sudan are not at all like the Trobriand Islanders of the Pacific; the ways of thought, or 'collective representation' as Durkheim calls them, of members of contemporary cultures may differ in quite fundamental and unexpected ways from our own.

It is difficult to see things as they are seen by members of another culture. It is not just a matter of "seeing the other fellow's point of view"; the problem is the very much more difficult one of comprehending the unacknowledged and unanalysed standpoint from which his views are derived. This is what is meant when it is said that the taken-for-granted commonsense view of the world must not be taken for granted but is itself the first subject for analytical investigation.

That goes for our own society. We are a savage tribe with strange customs and an inner system of mysterious drives of almost pathological significance.

Members of the Lugbara tribe of North-Western Uganda used to think that all foreigners were witches, dangerous and scarcely human creatures who walk about upside-down and kill people by magic. But that was how the sociologist Simmel came to see what he called "the topsy-turvy world of money", which is our particular form of life, and which turns people upside down and kills them with magic.

Durkheim's achievement was considerable; it formed the basis of the immense extension of anthropological work that went on through the twentieth century and passed far beyond the recording of the quaint customs of primitive people. For the first time it tried to get to the depths of *all* human societies. Once the key to human communities is found it could be applied to the more complex examples constituting all civilisations, including our own.

The same point of view was reached along a different route by Rickert in his search for the *ethos* of an historical society. Weber followed him in his own search for the understanding of capitalist society. He proceeds not by inductive reasoning from social facts, but by grasping the basic motivations, by understanding the nature of the 'group mind'. This same approach became the basis of the structural functionalism of Radcliffe Brown and Talcott Parsons.

We are now able to see that sociological concepts are not extracted from sense-experience or from our perception of the objects and persons of our environment. The compulsive hold they have over our thoughts cannot be explained in any such way. It is society, culture, the totality of custom and the practices of social tradition that are responsible for the conceptual forms in terms of which we apprehend society.

The importance of Durkheim lies in the priority he attaches to the *community*, by contrast to the individualist utilitarian theories prevalent from the time of John Locke to that of Bentham, Mill and the economists, which rooted society in the individual and the arrangements he made with other individuals so that each could pursue his personal ends. For these theories society was seen as a kind of contract, and law as the intervention of the policeman to prevent ill-disposed persons interfering with the normal process of legitimate personal end-seeking. Morals arose within the *individual* conscience and, if followed, created a good society; religious faith was found in *individual* hearts. The human will was exercised in each individual pursuing his personal aims.

Durkheim reversed all this. The individual was a manifestation of society, and could not exist unless created by it and functioning within it to preserve and maintain the social life of all. Our moral feelings are created in us by the needs of our fellows, our will is our recognition and obedience to what society demands of us. It is common social action, without which we can achieve nothing, not even keep alive, it is active co-operation, that creates a common consciousness. All beliefs, values, morals and ideas are held in common. All human behaviour emanates from or is conditioned by society. The moral order is neither a set of rules derived from the eternal principles of natural right, nor is it an agreed code designed to let us each pursue his individual aims in peace and security. It begins in society, in its norms, its rules, and its duties and obligations. Society, alone has the authority to create the sense of right.

Does this entirely absorb the individual into the 'group mind'? Not at all; there can be no society without the individuals that constitute it. The autonomy of each is manifested, not in the blind compulsion of the spirit of the hive, but only by the individual *understanding* that his own fulfilment is reached *only* in co-operation for a common good.

In human society the person knows what he has to do and why. It is never a matter of *submission* to the group, for in every man is both the man and the social being; man is "the ensemble of social relations". If our *social* feeling diminishes, our personality declines. If group support fails us and we feel isolated and alone, we move towards self-destruction (suicide); and group support varies inversely with the degree of social integration.

All our thinking, all our concepts, are derived from and *must* be derived from our co-operative social life. It is society, culture, the totality of custom and the practices of social traditions which inculcate and sustain our concepts, and make it impossible to escape them.[2]

The compulsive hold certain concepts have over our thoughts, but it does go beyond the simple acceptance of things, cannot be explained in these ways. There surface phenomena—and that is an important step. It are no *a priori* concepts, which are just there in the minds of stops there, however, with the problem only half all of us, nor, can they be extracted from sense-experience unravelled and *still* leaving us with an empirically observed as the empiricists suppose. social whole which Durkheim takes for granted.

How did this community come into being, and secondly This is by no means a completely satisfactory account of why is its unity constantly broken by the conflict between things, but it does go beyond the simple acceptance of the individuals and the State as representing the surface phenomena—and that is an important step. It community? Durkheim slides over these questions with stops there, however, with the problem only half the bland observation that all the obligations imposed on unravelled and *still* leaving us with an empirically observed individuals necessarily represent the welfare of the social whole which Durkheim takes for granted. community, the common good, and therefore there can be no grounds for conflict. When the individual protests that, How did this community come into being, and secondly on the contrary, his basic interests *are* being overridden, what are we to say? Durkheim gives no answer because he never raises the essential issue: that the conception of the State as representing the ideally rational community in which every constituent finds freedom and fulfilment may represent what society *ought* to be—but whether it is so in fact is open to question. To go on proclaiming that nevertheless such is the *reality* if only we could raise the level of our consciousness high enough to understand it, is simply to mask the real situation.

Refusing to go beyond the *actual* society with its unfulfilled ideals and basic conflicts is once again to take it as an already constituted society which we observe and describe but do not question or analyse. It simply accepts as given fact the totality of real social relationships obtaining in a given social group which can be directly observed as a system of regulative relationships, a *functioning* system and not merely a structure, and functioning to continue and maintain a particular pattern of *normative* conditions.

What Durkheim definitely adds to the value-free descriptions of the naïve descriptive sociology he found in existence, is the basic fact of values *incorporated* in the community. Society has a *collective conscience*, it creates in each individual a sense of *ought*, of duty, it imposes moral obligations, it creates a regulated and indeed coercive body of law to maintain the working of the system, to regulate it, to maintain it in equilibrium.

The conception of the maintenance by regulatory laws of existing values is a highly important idea. It must be accepted in matters of expectations and requirements, as also of the conduct of individuals in established relationships with one another and in allotted roles.

So far so good. But the concepts are still simply empirical, referring to the observable processes of social life *as it is*—but why as it *must* be? At this stage there is no analysis of existing phenomena to penetrate their inner nature or to ask how this society came to be. We do not strip away the outer forms in order to reveal the immanent structure of the real, but limit ourselves to an observable social order. Hence the unremitting emphasis on the normative arrangements of social systems by means of which orderly and workable systems of social relationships defined by social usage are made possible.

NOTES

1. The title of Emile Durkheim's "Elementary Forms of Religious Life" is misleading. It implies that the book is about primitive religion, whereas it is really about the nature of society.
2. Ernest Gellner, *Crisis in the Humanities.*

3

The Study of Cultures

Durkheim gives us only the externals of a functional society—its manifestations in all the varied activities of such a society. He dealt, indeed, with the determination of the parts by the whole; and Talcott Parsons later elaborated on internal structure and co-ordinating controls. But all this remains entirely on the surface. We never venture down into the dangerous region of reality.

Durkheim is telling us that our own society is really like a primitive society with its mass solidarity, its members sharing the tribal spirit. And Parsons elaborated the mechanism of all this. He did so with our own society very much in mind, and indicated its methods of unification and integration—above all of internalisation. They thus seem to move from the level of simple descriptions and classifications of the elements of our society to their organisation and synthesis and their subordination to an unstated goal or tribal spirit.

But all this remains no more than a structured elaboration of the society we belong to and observe, an insight into how it maintains its unity and achieve its goals. Analysed and focused thus, it impresses upon us the factual inescapability of the given social order. It is a mechanism and it confronts us.

The whole concept that is elaborated calls urgently for content, for substance. What exactly *is* the tribal spirit? What *is* that pervading attainment goal that rules all expectation patterns and all roles? We are not told. We must assume that the spirit and goals are those of our own society. Would the same structures and controls do for other societies? More importantly, what is the real essence of all the varied societies and what is their historical origin?

Moving parallel with these theories of the nature and structure of society was a totally different approach, not at all concerned with structure but very much concerned with the concrete substance of social life—its ethos, its spirit in its complete actuality. It arose in Germany during the last decade of the nineteenth century, in Heidelberg, where a group of scholars were developing the science of *culture* as contrasted with the science of *nature*.[1]

Kant had already laid it down that we order the objects of sense-experience into the system of natural laws by the built-in conceptual apparatus of the scientific reason. This, however, never gives us reality itself but only reality selected, organised and processed by the activity of the knowing mind. But, according to him, reality itself *can* be apprehended in its wholeness, as it really is, and in its own nature, as the world of values, the kingdom of ends; this is not by scientific reason but by the *practical* reason which apprehends its objects by direct intuition. This was argued as long ago as 1788; now a hundred years later it appeared in an entirely new form to establish the independence of sociology, the science of society, from natural science as a system of logically determined natural law, which, according to Kant, concerns only sense-experience, that is physical objects, and apprehends them as 'phenomena' according to the logical and mathematical categories of the physical sciences.

German intellectual life in the years before the first

world war was developing in a new way the distinction Kant had drawn between the scientific reason and the 'practical' reason which grasped ethical reality by intuition. The Heidelberg school of Neo-Kantians in particular sought to establish *historical* knowledge by a method of reasoning different from that of the generalising scientific method. Both Dilthey and Simmel represented a reaction against positivism, and especially against all theories which denied the possibility of insight into the nature of reality. Heinrich Rickert of Heidelberg became the most influential of these philosophers to whom history was the knowledge of what is unique, specific and individual as opposed to the abstract, general laws of natural science. Rickert argued that the human material of history and culture could not be comprehended by the methods of generalising natural science. We need another kind of reason, akin to Kant's 'practical reason', to grasp by intuition the spirit of a human culture which is not subject to the logical categories. This he called *Verstehen*, 'understanding'; and by it we can grasp the *unique* forms of human culture as they arise in history. Unlike the material natural science handles, which is the same everywhere and can be comprehended in universal laws covering all space and time, human culture appears in an infinite variety of different types each one of which has to be grasped by a *particular* understanding of its own uniqueness. What is thus grasped is a *life style*, a special form of human living, its modes of thought, its ethical norms, its aesthetic achievements.

Dilthey's task was to explore the wide range of historical cultures in this spirit, to show each as a quite independent and unique type of living with its own values, institutions, art, morals and ways of living—very much as Toynbee describes each of the twenty-two distinct civilisations he finds in history. These types of culture with their specific values, proceeding from the inner mental life whose expressions they are, can be seen as Life Philosophies, or World Views, in concrete historical forms. They are not, as for Hegel, the unfolding of the *Idea*, but simply the *historical specificity* of different types of society and civilisation appearing in special circumstances, places and times. Thus the civilisation of China is unique, as is that of the Graeco-Roman world and, of course, the later form of European history including our own.

Each type has to be apprehended in its uniqueness by an intuitive recognition of its specific character, and the faculty by which we do this is not the faculty with which we comprehend scientific truth. Rickert, Dilthey and their school thus establish a mode of historical being, that of human culture, or the *human* sciences, which we grasp with a type of understanding and by methods of its own.

This became the basis of Weber's 'ideal type', which was not an hypothesis to explain the given facts of capitalist society but the intuitive perception of 'the spirit of capitalism'. The existing system is grasped as a *Weltanschauung*, a World View, something unique. It is not understood in terms of any generalisation about society as such. Thus it is clear that Weber's sociology does not claim to successfully cover the Indian Caste system, Chinese élitism, Greek ruling-class democracy on a basis of slavery, or the medieval feudal system. And clearly Parsons, for his part, had industrial society in the United States at the back of his mind, and nothing else. It would seem, then, that a separate formal organisation would be needed for each type of society. What would this imply? A series of discrete social orders, each a structural-functional system and each confronting its members as a given pre-constituted and unalterable entity.

One may perhaps go farther. Historical inquiry does indicate a recognisable uniqueness in the distinct civilisations known to us, and Toynbee and Spengler have helped us to see that we must not attempt to grasp other societies in terms of the special concepts of our own. Can we ever really put ourselves in the place of the inhabitants of that Roman society which, beneath the noble architecture and competent organisation of its State and legal institutions, was a society peopled with malign supernatural forces, demons and numina of darkness and mystery which the atheist Lucretius thought it were well to rid the world of? Consider the gulf between medieval supernaturalism and ecclesiastical pretensions and the cool negative rationalism of the eighteenth century of Voltaire and Diderot.

This raises a crucial question that never occurred to Rickert or Dilthey, or later still to Weber. It is surely strange if human social history is constituted by the succession and co-existence of a multitude of incommensurate 'life forms', each of which can only be apprehended by an intuition which grasps its uniqueness by immediate *Verstehen*. Is an ultimate pluralism the last word?

It would appear at once that if Dilthey presents us with a reified absolute, we are now presented (if Toynbee's count of civilisations is accurate) with twenty-two more; for each will require its own type of structure and organisation. It is difficult to see where in all this a single science of society is possible. On the contrary, it lands us in an arbitrary world of total relativity, for which no scientifically constructed theory is or ever will be available.

However, Weber made excellent use of the Rickert–Dilthey approach. He applied it to one system in particular—industrial capitalism, just as Parsons applied his organisational forms to it later. But Weber looked for the unique constituting spirit, the historical specificity of capitalism, and found it in its basic economic motivation and goal. This became the organising principle which created the structure and function. No doubt Parsons could offer his abstract scheme for the purpose, but Weber's own model grows out of the very spirit of capitalism itself.

The Rickert–Dilthey recourse to the special types of society which emerge in history might, indeed, offer us something more than a limited sociology of capitalism; but where it fails is in the arbitrariness of the appearance of all the many different types of society. Where do they come from, and why? How do they arise? Nor is there any suggestion of their changing and developing, or having developed from other forms. That being so, they simply confront us, as every empiricism is confronted, with *the thing as it is*, pre-constituted, finished, and to be accepted without question. We are back where we started, with the arbitrary authority of the 'given'. This is not the answer, not a real theory or science of society; it achieves no more than to pose the still unexamined problem.

Each successive theory from Durkheim onwards only extends the notion of a fixed order. At first, as the naïve empiricist sees it, not much more than a catalogue of social phenomena; then a society expressing and dominated by the collective spirit; after that the self-regulating equilibrium in which the individual is controlled like the toothed wheels in the mechanism of a clock; finally each society is said to represent a unique culture pattern.

As we ourselves see society, with our own vision, from our own stance, it shows us the order of our own system of society, which for us is *given*, all that is or can be, a structural and functional but also a spiritual determinism. It presents us with the finality and absoluteness of the order in which we find ourselves. It is constructed to control the expectations of each one of us, to prescribe the limits of our aspiration, *internalising* the culture and spirit of the hive so that the pattern and goal are steadfastly followed.

Two questions are *never* asked, are indeed held to be meaningless: How did this come to be? And must it remain as it is? These, we are told, are *metaphysical* questions. Did not Kant point out that the very principle and way of our knowing precludes anything more than the discovery of the interior logic of the given system and its determinism? This is exhaustive of what can be known, it marks the limits of the rational, the meaningful, the knowable.

Dilthey reminds us that there is nothing in any sociology of any particular society to give us the sense of a common human destiny, the growth of society as such, or any goal which man is seeking. There can be as many totally different social systems as you like, with different aims, goals and rules. Whatever *is* is given, and we accept it. This was undoubtedly how in past ages people saw themselves; but with the dawn of science, the study of history, after the period of the Enlightenment, we have come to see the destiny of man as one story of development and achievement, with whatever set-backs and periods of stagnation and regression there may certainly have been. Those who agree with Dilthey can have no philosophy of man. A total relativism takes the meaning out of history and out of life, it denies the superiority of any one line of development over others and therefore of any sense of value or direction for our own society as well as for others.

Men sail a boundless and bottomless sea; there is neither harbour for shelter nor floor for anchorage, neither starting place nor appointed destination.[2]

When we consider the type of society the sociologists offer us as the unchangeable pattern of our lives we may wonder whether there is really no alternative, no future possibilities.

There is no hint of anything particularly unpleasant in Durkheim's description of a beautifully integrated community; but there definitely is in Talcott Parsons', where for the first time we hear of 'deviance', of 'internalising' obedience and submission, to, in the last resort, the arm of the law. For 'deviance' read 'rebellion', for 'internalising' read 'brain-washing' and indoctrination. Dilthey unwittingly opens the window on other vistas. In one's own society, perhaps, acquiescence is 'internalised', rebellion *can* be proclaimed pathological, 'deviance' provides a satisfying word that removes anxiety or even feelings of guilt. Here all may still be for the best in the best of all possible worlds. But there are other civilisations, other societies, on which we can look with a more candid eye. Weber, the immediate successor of Dilthey, bids us look at India and China; at rigid caste systems with their millions condemned to servile status or without even that status—out-caste; at the established, authoritative élitism of the mandarin lords of old China.

When we take such a look around, then a new word appears in sociology; *domination*—and the word is Weber's. It is also the unspoken word for Talcott Parsons' regulatory mechanism and Durkheim's group mind. And it fits the society which is the present object of sociology, the social world-for-us, the given culture in which we live and move and have our being. This first became immediately apparent before Weber had written a word about 'the spirit of capitalism'.

It seemed to many at the turn of the century that society as it was could not be questioned. Its origin was not investigated nor its further development considered as a possibility. On the contrary, for the social philosopher society had to be taken as it was, as the world as it is for us—in good Kantian terms. But just for these reasons its actual nature, though accepted, awakened the gravest misgivings in the minds of some thinkers closely associated with the Dilthey and Rickert tradition.

Ferdinand Tönnies' work *Gemeinschaft und Gesellschaft*, although published in 1887, was rediscovered and again published in 1912, and became widely known in the growing mood of scepticism that followed the first world war. It struck a note subsequently to be deepened and intensified in the work of Weber. Tönnies saw that there was indeed something unique about contemporary capitalist culture, and its unique character was an unpleasant one.

The pattern that appeared as the spirit of the age was one that substituted individualism, impersonality, hard bargaining, and egoism (*Gesellschaft*) for the community spirit of mutuality and recognition of the person belonging to *Gemeinschaft*. By *Gemeinschaft* Tönnies meant the spirit of fellowship, of community, in the old society before the coming of the spirit of individualism characteristic of the new Germany, the *Gesellschaft* manifested in its purest form in capitalist economics and commercial law. In its beginning this seems to mean nothing but progress, but in fact it means the loss of community feeling. Here "everybody is by himself and isolated, and there exists a condition of tension against all others".[3] If this is society as it has to be, then we must resign ourselves to living in a depersonalised world.

Georg Simmel who died in 1918, was closely associated with the Heidelberg group and with both Rickert and Weber. And like Tönnies he was acutely aware of something destructive of personality in the capitalist world, but accepted it as a fact of life. Empiricism now became the recognition and acceptance in the common-sense world of a destructive element.

The deepest problems of modern life derive from the claim of the individual to preserve the autonomy and individuality of his existence in the face of overwhelming forces, of historical heritage, of external culture, and of the technique of life. The fight with nature which primitive man has to wage for his bodily existence attains in this modern form its latest transformation.[4]

Neither Tönnies nor Simmel are criticising capitalism as socialists; for them this *is* the empirical world—and it is a very nasty one. Simmel even thought it a good thing that we should have to face the destructive pressures of society, for then we are compelled to reassert personality. But neither of them could envisage any alternative. This was society, and it was implacably unalterably hostile to man.

We have come a long way from Durkheim and Dilthey. Neither of them even thought of investigating what we now call the sub-structure of their unified societies, its economy; there is no suggestion that they ever imagined that society could have a sub-structure. Nor did they ever raise the question of the exact nature of the group need, of the all-pervading, all-controlling cultural ethos of their unique society. It is Weber's distinction that he did raise this question. But he answered it, not by pointing to an historically constituted economic sub-structure *in* our society, but rather in terms of the constituting 'spirit' of its structure and its functioning in every part. The ethos of our culture was in his own words 'the spirit of capitalism'. This, he said, was associated with and rested upon a given economic sub-structure which determined its totality, that is to say all its institutions and social forms.

Weber thus sought to fill the yawning gap in the empiricist sociology of the nineteenth century. He explained the *basis* of that society in its *uniqueness*, showing exactly what *is* given, pre-constituted, what we take for granted and accept as our fate as the nature of things. But for Weber, who could no more see beyond the given than Durkheim, or Dilthey, or Talcott Parsons, it was nothing to be complacent about; it was a depressing and altogether unhappy state of affairs.

NOTES

1. H. Rickert, *Kulturwissenschaft und Naturwissenschaft.*
2. M. Oakeshott, *Inaugural Lecture at the London School of Economics.*
3. F. Tönnies, *Fundamental Concepts.*
4. G. Simmel, *Die Grosstädte und das Geisterleben.*

'The God of Things as They Are'

At the end of the nineteenth century the advanced countries of Western Europe and America were well satisfied with themselves. The revolutions of 1848 were matters of the past. The present appeared to be an age of progress and stable constitutional government.

Nevertheless, industrialisation had created as much poverty at one end of the social scale as riches at the other; and, in a manner not anticipated by the economists, had been driven by the need for expansion to extend its colonial empires in Africa and the East.

Weber appears as a typical representative of the dominant and self-confident business community in the academic world of philosophy and economic theory. An academic, most certainly. But the professorial attitude was replaced by something unusual in university circles —passionate conviction, and the sense of a vocation to toughen the fibre of contemporary capitalism, refute its critics and above all renew the spirit of modern Germany. He appears as the vehement, committed exponent of the economic and political system, and the severe critic of attempts to interfere with its operations on the basis of ethical judgements which he regarded as utopian and subjective.

There was more reason for this intervention than appeared on the surface. There was a growing economic demand, arising from the rapid development of German industry, for access to new markets and raw materials, for expansion and capital investment beyond the German Reich. German expansion had begun much later than that of Britain and France; huge areas of the world in Asia and Africa had in the nineteenth century fallen within the political and economic sphere of the two Great Powers, leaving the rapidly expanding and ambitious German industrial system demanding a redivision of the colonial world and her 'place in the sun'.

There had also arisen alongside her industrial development and as part of it a powerful working-class trade union and political movement, well organised and led, inspired by the teachings of Karl Marx—a man who was by no means a utopian, but an able economist and a reputable philosopher who had won the respect, if not the agreement, of much of the German academic world. Abroad, Labriola and Croce, eminent Italian scholars, supported his views; in Germany Karl Kautsky and Franz Mehring were among the able and highly educated theorists who led the German Social Democratic Party; while the economic theories of Werner Sombart and Hilferding owed much to the influence of *Capital*.

Weber early recognised that Marxism was a serious threat to German capitalism. It was to be combated neither by Bismarckian repression nor by derision, but by demolishing its theoretical basis on the one hand and supporting capitalism with an organised scientific theory on the other.

Weber's philosophy was in sharp distinction from the views of those traditional thinkers whose ideas were exclusively an individual expression of the concrete swamped in a complex of abstractions—a philosopher's philosophy that touched life hardly at all. Weber gave expression to the conception of the world held by a multitude of people, maintaining an overall trend and standard of collective action. His philosophy was part of living history. It not only expressed the life, the energy, and the ideals of his world, it sought to explain it, to make it conscious of itself. It was as strictly an empirical sociology as academic philosophy was speculative. For it attempted to establish a science of social fact, and to use an appropriate methodology devised for historico-political material rather than for the natural sciences, a methodology which would describe and classify historical and social facts schematically and deduce experimentally the laws-system of society. Being an empiricist venture, based on directly presented data, it neither required further explanation as to its meaning, nor was any such explanation possible. The data needed only to be described and analysed. The theory dealt simply with 'whatever is the case', and made no attempt to penetrate into the essence of phenomena or to find behind them some ultimate 'meaning',—a process which was rejected as metaphysical.

Weber's sociology tried to grasp capitalist society as a whole, and to see its laws and institutions as reflecting the acquisitive spirit of capitalism. He took society as he found it and endeavoured to systematise the institutions, the economic structure, and the social behaviour-patterns of society as immediately observed reality. It appeared that nothing could be more objective and therefore certain than a science based on the evidence of observation.

But both in the natural sciences and in sociology direct perception is deceptive, leading to the view that we are confronted with something which is *in itself* just what it appears to be. This is by no means the case and has long ago been rejected by the physical sciences, and it would be interesting to find out why it is still virtually unchallenged in sociology.

The naïve realism which accepts the immediate impression of experiences as unquestionable truth has been challenged by every philosopher since John Locke and was rejected by both Marx and Lenin. This attitude was well described by Collingwood as "the lowest type of low-grade thinking, thinking at almost zero level—low-grade routinised thought, so casual and haphazard that it is hardly thinking at all".[1] To take what immediately confronts us, either in science of sociology, unhistorically, uncritically, with the unshakeable conviction that things must be as they seem to be, is a philosophy one can only equate with stupidity and dogmatism.

In sociology we not only have to accept the limitations of observations which are likely to be more biased than in natural science, and the impossibility of using scientific method based on repeated experiment. We cannot, as is the case in natural science, take for granted the availability of a pre-constituted world of phenomena for investigation. We do not have to ask of the natural world how and why it came to be constituted, nor are we concerned with the possibility of, say, the sudden disappearance of the law of gravity or of a revolution in the valency law on which chemistry is based. Social order is the emergent product of human activity. And the essential question it poses concerns *how* it arose, and whether it is going to continue in the same way. This is a totally different attitude from that with which we approach astronomy and physics, which deal with a self-sufficient world, independent of man, *out there.*

The first requirement for the analysis of the nature of the social order must be to regard it as itself problematic. And this implies a suspension of belief in the facticity of that order, so as to concentrate on its historical origin, the conditions under which it was constructed, and the intention and aims embodied in it.

This approach contrasts with both the 'mindless empiricism' which believes in no theorising at all and falls into the error of illegitimate reification of a given social order, and the later system of Weber, who sees society as the emergent network of orderly close relationships, demonstrated in a sociology which tries to grasp in the reality of the group mind the nature of society as a whole. Weber's approach is, indeed, a great improvement on any mere description of society as we observe it; but it still takes the conceptual system for reality, in spite of the fact that it is manifestly an abstract construction, and inevitably based on the presuppositions of the sociologists.

The moment we fit reality into a preconceived pattern we are in certain danger of the fallacy of *misplaced concreteness*, for the social system is now treated as if it were *really* the preconceived closely organised system. We convert its internal logic into the laws of a highly structural order, all procedures to study which are *deductive*; that is to say, everything in society is shown to follow logically from its structure. But society is a process and not a system of structures corresponding to abstract concepts; it is in continuous change, and can and does change from one pattern or system to a totally different one.

A genuine sociology will lay the whole emphasis not on existing structure and its mechanism, as though sociology can know but one form of society, that which now exists, but on the process of world-building, men making use of nature, men as conscious creative agents making their own economic systems and civilisations. This sees men belonging to a fellowship of humanity.

We understand, we plan, we co-operate, we organise. But we are never finally subjected to our own organisation. We made it, and we can take it to pieces and reconstruct it. Such sociology will be concerned with the work of the self and others in a world held in common.

It is often difficult for us to understand that any other world than our own could really be possible, has ever existed in the past, or could ever exist in the future. When we dress characters up in space gear and send them voyaging through space to other worlds, apart from some pretentious posing for the TV they act in ways perfectly comprehensible to us. Even our villains are villains because they set at nought our conventional moral codes. If, on the other hand, we re-construct the romances of the past, of Elizabethan England or or of ancient Baghdad, we still tend to think of the people in the same way, as just ourselves in fancy dress and pretending to speak in Shakespearian language or in that of the Arabian Nights. Our utopias are artificial reconstructions of bourgeois society with the unpleasant things left out, whether we are reading H. G. Wells's *Modern Utopia*, William Morris's *News from Nowhere* or Edward Bellamy's *Looking Backward*.

The real scholars know better. What can we—scientists, historians, philosophers—of the twentieth century make of the world of ideas and values and conceptions of the thirteenth century? We attempt to translate it into modern terms, but in the climate of opinion represented by 'their' philosophy, 'their' science, and 'their' religion, we can only gasp for breath. The world pattern into which they are woven is no longer capable of being comprehended by our mentality.

Our society, our world, our ideology is not the only one in existence, nor has it always been the way of life of our people. The ideology of England of 1675 was very different from that of 1975, and will certainly be as alien to our descendants in the twenty-first century as the seventeenth century is to us. This would certainly be the view they will take of our present topsy-turvy world of economic crisis, and of the strangely distorted and perverted literature and drama of our present unrest and confusion—a world whose objective limitations prevent us housing our people, keeping our currencies stable, and paying our nurses and teachers a decent wage, in spite of being one of the wealthiest countries of the world with a democractic constitution, all the blessings of a free society, and an incorruptible Civil Service. All this seems common sense and good sense to us, but it will be seen as a form of mental derangement in a hundred years' time.

History compels us to understand that world views are never as permanent and the objectives of belief never so absolute in their metaphysical reality and authority as men in different ages always believe. Common sense becomes uncommon nonsense within little more than a century. Galileo, Descartes and Newton broke up the medieval synthesis which had dominated the mind of Europe since the thirteenth century; Darwin's theory of evolution revolutionised biology. In social thinking there have been similar upheavals. The peasant and craft economy of the middle ages, with its guilds of city merchants, has given place to an industrial society run by bankers. What now dawns upon us as readers of the daily papers, viewers of TV or uneasy first-year students fresh from the narrow limits of the sixth forms, is that our whole way of thinking, our conceptions of the world, the ordinary common sense of the man in the street, in the pub bar, at the club, in the Common Room, has really been *imposed* upon us. We wonder whether, after all, we should accept the imprint of such conventional outside influences on the moulding of our personalities. There arises a sudden determination to begin to think critically about our society, to ask how its notions, customs, moral rules, economic limitations and classes came to be; and who are responsible for them.

But what has been called 'mindless empiricism', and likewise the 'group mind' sociology of Durkheim, Dilthey and Weber, takes the given structure of society as we find it very much for granted. The 'world-view' theorists did at least see society as an organised whole with a unique culture—its own 'spirit', which was responsible for all its institutions, its economy and its values. But they saw this quite unhistorically and without any attempt to explain its place in the sequence of social systems, least of all to envisage its supersession.

What they took for granted would be rather taken by a

scientific sociology as posing the basic question. And this makes the beginning of a genuine science of society, a sociology going beyond the pattern of the ready-made thinking imposed on us. It may not be 'common sense' but it is good sense. It is not a sociology dragging us along by the trends and forces and ideas of our time and submitting us to its economic and social compulsions, but a social science that begins by asking *why* things are so, and continues by inquiring into the historical origins of our society *and the trends that point beyond it*. The great danger in accepting this, suggests one anxious social theorist, is that it may lead to our 'sliding into Marxism'.

Weber appears at the very moment of challenge to the old order. We find the social philosophers and sociologists in two camps; the one party accepting things as they are without question, accepting a self-justifying sociology for a value-free economy, accepting the 'given' of the current bourgeois world with its unconditional necessities; the other party challenging its assumptions, the finality of its concepts and of its law systems.

Marx died when Weber was a university student aged nineteen. *Capital* was exercising its growing influence as he grew up. It was being widely read and discussed in the academic world of Germany, and had already become the bible of a powerful and growing working-class party. In his maturity Weber felt it his mission to challenge the whole ideology of Marxism and to defend existing society and its institutions against it. He achieved this not only by his theoretical work but by his advocacy of the consolidation of the State, by his political addresses designed to steel the nerves of Germany to endure the strains of maintaining the economy and extending the political and economic power beyond its present frontiers. He reproached the critics and waverers for sentimental utopianism, and the moralists for their subjective illusions. Above all he met his opponents with a philosophy which confounded their arguments and provided the German bourgeoisie with a powerful defence of their entire social system, its economy, its bureaucratic establishment, its State power, its moral certainties, and its cultural principles. He did this in a work of close argument and considerable logical power, his *Methodology of the Social Sciences*.

NOTE

1. R. G. Collingwood, *An Essay on Metaphysics*.

5

Weber's Methodology

Empiricist thinking, the attitude which takes for granted what *is*, what confronts us, as sheer fact, does not ask *why* things are so. The facts of life are, as they say, *contingent*, which means that they could be otherwise but happen to be just what they are. A flower is blue; but flowers are of all colours and it does not matter to the flower whether it is red, blue or yellow: some flowers are even green. There is no reason why it *must* be blue. Other things, on the contrary, *must* be as they are, there is a reason why they have to be so, these phenomena, we say, are not contingent but *necessary*. If this is a metal it *must* transmit electricity. If this is water it *must* be reducible to hydrogen and oxygen. These are consequences that we know *must* follow. We know it *before* it happens. Contingent facts do not have to be so; we know *what* they are only by waiting until experience shows us how they happen to turn out.

Dilthey and Rickert saw the uniqueness of every society as simply given, as undeniable and inescapable fact. Social reality, human reality, is quite different in this respect from anything studied by natural science. In nature everything is explicable in terms of law: it has to be; it is determined causally. In history there are no recurrent and invariable sequences repeated again and again. Things happen only *once*, and do not happen again in exactly the same way. So, it was concluded, a particular society, whether Chinese or Indian or Sioux or Azande, or feudal or that of modern capitalism, does not *have* to be like it is; it is like a flower of a particular colour, and there is nothing more to be said except to make an exhaustive analysis of just what it *is*, in all its remarkable *differences* from other societies or other civilisations.

Durkheim got no farther than postulating a distinctive 'group mind' which was responsible for the manifest behaviour, characteristics and beliefs of the members of society; and the functionalist Parsons no further than postulating that the unique whole implied a complex structure of interacting units maintaining a certain equilibrium. But for both of them this analysis was merely a general description of a given and contingent fact. It could have been otherwise. Our capitalist system or the medieval feudal system just *happen* to be so. We take them for granted and do not ask why; for one does not ask 'why' of the contingent facts of life. The functionalist only explains that the organisation is necessary, the rules operate, the machinery is constructed in this or that elaborate way, to maintain and sustain the behaviour, the institutions, the characteristics of this or that unique society. But he does not go farther. Society in the form of a particular complex organisation is still only a contingent fact.

Weber appears at this point to take the matter a good deal farther, but not by any means to the end of the road. As a disciple and friend of Rickert he had been taught that any society, including our own, exhibits a unique form of its own whose special nature is to be grasped by intuitive knowledge. We have to *see* just what kind of society it is. Weber was the first of the 'culture philosophers' to ask *what exactly* our capitalist society is, not just in its organisation but in *the purpose and motivation* that the organisation comes into existence to sustain. He therefore asks *why* it has this capitalist structure; what capitalism is striving for; what its motivation amounts to; what is the mainspring of its whole system of economic law, customs, institutions, laws and political organisation.

It might be thought that a straightforward description of the economic system would give the necessary content to the organisational structure of society in terms of a scientific system of economic laws; but the Heidelberg philosophers did not regard anything connected with the human side of existence, with its immense variety of aims, motives, feelings and values, as explicable in the same terms as in the physical sciences. Weber agreed with them. He was convinced of the inadequacy of empirical observation and its generalisations to explain the nature of any such historical order as modern capitalism.

He had discovered a totally different method of how to get at the essential nature of a society composed of men, not things. What he had to explain was a world of motives and values that natural science never even looks at. He got the clue to the problem from the method Kant adopted in relation to natural law. Weber's master stroke was to apply the Kantian method to society.

Kant did not believe that by observing physical data an explanatory law system could be extracted by induction or any such rational process. We reach an explanation in terms of 'laws' by applying a preconceived conceptual form to the data. He knew that by doing so he had not reached reality as it is *in itself*, but only a synthesis of the evidence which gives us reality as it is *for us*. Kant then arrived at the world of values by another route altogether, by an intuitive act which reached reality itself as moral law. We are not concerned with that for the moment; but with Weber's adaptation of the Kantian method beyond the world of physical science, to history and society.

What he did was to construct an interpretative scheme, as an explanatory model, and use it to make sense of the facts.

This model is not only concerned with the economy but with the purpose it serves, with the motivation of our society. In natural science we do not have to look for motives: physical events are not purposeful. But with society, motivation is the really important thing. It enables us to grasp the real essence of a human association and to understand the meaning of what its members are doing. Weber's model embraces the economy, and the whole pattern of social behaviour associated with it, in terms of its fundamental motivation.

A mechanical system as explained by the natural sciences is concerned with antecedent physical conditions and elements and their calculable resultant. Determination is from behind, is in what has happened *before* the event. It is the past that creates the present. But in human affairs the event, while dependent upon physical causation, is itself determined by what does not yet exist as a material fact, but only as an idea, or intention, or purpose in the mind. It is determined by the prevision of what has not yet occurred and does not yet exist as a fact.

On this basis, never falling back into mechanistic materialism, working with individual motivations and the intelligence of the human mind, Weber constructs his model of a whole type of society—its economic organisation, its administering bureaucracy, its system of government and law; using as many additional sub-types as necessary. In this way he is able to create a really 'human' science of society, or sociology, and not a system of physics masquerading as one.

What science had to get rid of before it could become science at all was the notion of final causes in nature. This was condemned as animism, as finalism. Weber, however, operates with final causes, but not of an animistic or mystical nature, but those of human purposes and human goal-seeking: and this, and nothing less, is for him the basis of all human behaviour.

There is therefore never *one* regular pattern of social

events, as in physics or chemistry, and no scientific system inductively based on the endless repetition of the same causes and the same effects is possible. Human life is endlessly varied and changing and novel events are always happening. People are not machines following repetitive sequences of predetermined actions, they follow their own changing motives and intentions. All social phenomena reveal people pursuing ends, holding different values and so behaving differently. Therefore *knowledge* of society, which means knowledge of human behaviour, must depend not on this behaviour falling always into fixed patterns, as is the case in electricity, or chemistry, but depends on our guessing or knowing its *motivation*. Only if one knows that can one understand anything going on in society.⌐

It is in this way that Weber seeks to understand society. Among all the motives actuating people and all the various goals they seek, can he discern a pattern of living that covers the whole area of human life *in our particular society*, and at this moment in history? For Weber would agree entirely with Dilthey that there have been and may still be many totally different types of society. ⌐It is because Durkheim's very general idea of a 'group mind', a 'collective form', is entirely empty of content, purely abstract, that it doesn't really help us.⌐ The same is true about any purely general system of structural organisation. There can in fact be no general formal system, for everything depends on the *particular* motivation of a particular society, and that is totally different in different ages and places. What Weber sets out to do is to find the basic goals and motivation of society as he finds it in Germany and Western Europe at the end of the nineteenth century. What is it that here and now makes people tick? What are they after in our day and age?

For Weber this means that looking at people and their busy lives we want to discover what intentions they have, what goals they are seeking, what their values are; and we must select those types of action for study which are explained by these motives and intentions, which reveal their meaning.

This *selected* motivation, working with rationally selected means, gives us a certain *type* of human behaviour. And on this basis we proceed to create what in the sciences is nowadays called a *model*, and what Weber calls an 'ideal type'. This becomes the pattern of the whole given society and all its activities, and gives us the key to the understanding of our particular society. What emerges out of the tangled web of behaviour-patterns and infinitely diversified social phenomena is *our* culture pattern.

Such a culture is a finite segment of the meaningless infinity of the world process, a segment on which human beings confer meaning and significance.[1]

It is important to understand that this is one man's guess as to what that pattern of living is. It is Max Weber's, and he never pretends that it is anything more than his subjective choice of a culture pattern. It will be justified entirely by the fact that it turns out to be useful when we use it to get a grip on the facts, that it really does make sense of things.

It is hypothetical. It is *not* a generalisation deemed established because it is verified by all the facts. It is *not* advanced as a theory of social life as a whole. It is simply a pattern of society which makes sense of our experience, of our own and other people's lives in our own society. It is an *as if* theory. *If* this were a true model, then people would be likely to behave in certain ways. They *do* in fact behave *as if* this were the case. As a model it has no other reason for being regarded as up to a point true, or likely.

Weber makes no attempt to conceal or evade the fact that this 'ideal type' emerges from his own value-oriented approach which determines *what* is selected for examination and the direction of the constructive process which follows. Weber's whole theory, flatly rejecting the naïve view that one's theory is derived from an objective appreciation of the facts, discloses (in Kantian fashion, and correctly) that we cannot but see our world through the grid of our presuppositions, our class, our interests, the society of which we are members. Like Durkheim, he sees our knowing mind in its conceptual forms and selective bias as constituted by the society itself of which our thinking is a manifestation and expression.

What, then, is the grid, the conceptual form, the whole stance and way of life which is the basis and determining approach of Weber's sociology? As we have seen, it comprises the outlook, the prejudices, the values, of a typical member of the upper class of the German business community. Weber not only knows this, but he goes out of his way to explain that his selection of a model, of a chosen motivation for our society, is entirely determined by his own personal approach, by his values, his standpoint. What he is saying is: it would be foolish and dishonest to pretend that there can be objectivity and neutrality in the point of view from which we construct our science of society. So we choose to be completely frank about it, with ourselves, and with everybody. We openly state our subjective bias. But you may find that it is a very useful point of view all the same, if, in fact, it works. Our model, our choice of the basic motivation of society is, admittedly, 'value-oriented'; but when we have got it, *then* we shall be ruthlessly objective in showing exactly how it works, what its natural logic really is. Here we shall not allow any outside interference by subjective moral standards to have any validity. The *logic* of our chosen motivation system is what is value free.

The model is called by Weber an 'ideal type' and he is perfectly aware that others would select different facts guided by other motives, and present quite a different picture of society.

By 'ideal' he does not mean that this type is in his

view desirable, or excellent, or the best of its kind. It is just roughly typical of a certain kind of living and acting. In fact it is never perfectly exemplified in reality, any more than one can ever draw a perfectly straight line or circle.

Having selected our type or model, we are able to work out its principles in a rational way. What is central is the goal-direction. This is its value motivation. It is a complete mistake to imagine that Weber excludes values from his system. On the contrary, it is a value-controlled form of life and nothing else. What he objects to is that, having constructed our model, we then judge its working by an outside and different value system which could have been the inner goal motivation and principle of quite another model. We shall therefore work out for *our* model the rational means to *its* chosen end in the light of all the foreseeable consequences, and *that* will be our only criterion, our only rule: namely, does the operation of these means attain the chosen ends?

It is important to understand that the method adopted is not the kind of generalisation that in the natural sciences we arrive at by induction from the facts. Weber rejects the inductive method for the social sciences. His is a *pragmatic* solution, chosen because we believe that it will work, retained so long as it does appear to work.

The fact that the model takes an economic form does not mean that Weber's *ideal type* is an economic model of capitalism. It is a model of Western society today, and of the whole of that society, of its very essence. It is in fact a capitalist society, and that is the important thing about it. This means that while people could conceive of capitalism *in* our society, or in any kind of society, and also conceive of our society running its economy on another model, that is not how Weber sees it. Our society itself has come into existence as part of, as dependent upon, and as constituted by capitalism. Capitalism is unthinkable without the society it has created and all its institutions, laws and rules:

and our society is unthinkable, for the same reason, apart from the spirit, the motive, the organs, the form of government, the bureaucracy of capitalism.

We have used the term 'model' as a near synonym of 'ideal type'. There are four useful terms which are not quite parallel: *type*, *model*, *paradigm* and *hypothesis*. But a 'hypothesis', as a theory about some aspect of nature or society, implies a certain tentativeness and distance from what it explains. A 'type' covers the whole object to be described and the word 'typical' usefully indicates what it tries to do. A 'model' means a construction, real or imaginary, in which something complex is rendered understandable—or, as is usually the case in scientific investigation, which is used to clarify a very complex reality by incorporating in workable form the *essential* features of the system under examination.

Weber uses his 'ideal type' by no means simply to model society or capitalism. It is a method that can be used to model all sorts of things. We could work out a model for a *bureaucracy*, as made up of certain elements of organisation ordered in degrees of authority from the top downwards, of its specialised function, its principle of responsibility to the official next above, its rules of procedure and so forth. It could be used to describe types of religion: Protestantism, Buddhism and so forth, or forms of government, or systems of law, or types of value: absolute values, traditional values, emotional values, values operating with rational choice of means.

Weber constantly reminds us, incidentally, that a type is never perfectly realised in fact, but it is indispensable for understanding the examples which never actually conform to it. An excellent type of this sort is 'the typical chordate', which is essential for the understanding of animal morphology from the fish to the vertebrates. But actually there is no 'typical chordate'.

Models are essential to the natural sciences as well as to social thinking. There was the Ptolemaic model of the universe with the Earth as the fixed centre around which sun, moon, planets, and stars revolved in concentric spheres. This was succeeded by the well-known Copernican model. There have been many models of the action of the heart, of combustion, of heat, of light (is it a wave or a particle, or both?). There have been successive models of the atom (earlier ones were soon discarded as inadequate), and of electricity (for which one of the last models took the form of Clerk Maxwell's equations expressing the fundamental electro-magnetic laws in terms of the electrical and magnetic properties of any given medium). For a last example we have Crick and Watson's double-helix model of the DNA molecule—one of the most brilliant and difficult conceptions ever devised by scientific thought. This again is a *model*.

What Kuhn has called a *paradigm* is another kind of model.[2] A typical paradigm in grammar consists of the most general forms of a verb, declined in all its moods, tenses and persons. It can then serve as a model from which irregular verbs derivate, and so as a basic framework for all the verbal forms in the language. The importance of a paradigm for science is that it indicates the total form of all thinking over a very wide field. It is therefore more than a type, and more than a model. The Darwinian discovery of evolution gives us a new *paradigm* within which all biological thinking now proceeds. The Copernican paradigm succeeded the Ptolemaic, and the Einsteinean paradigm that of Newton. Each change is of the nature of a revolution, a drastic re-ordering of the whole mental world, its viewpoint, its concepts, its *language*. Kuhn considered this a matter of the first importance, because it means that if we accept a paradigm it becomes for us *reality itself*, our Kantian conceptual form in which we have to do all our thinking, and we cannot think in any other terms. Weber sees his "ideal type" as the *paradigm* of the form of life, the universe of discourse, the language, of our society: and it means that we cannot easily (although we think we can) think ourselves into a pre-capitalist or a *post-capitalist* world.

Recent theories about language have introduced a further concept to those of model and paradigm, that of 'language games'. It has been realised that language is not a simple matter of picturing objects—a word for each thing, its label. Language has a descriptive function, of course, but its range and importance goes far beyond that. It is primarily concerned with fields of action and with forms of life. There are various activities, for instance, which we know as 'games', like cricket, chess or golf. For each there is a set of rules and given entities (chessmen, goals, stumps, wicket-keepers, putting greens) which together with the rules constitute a special rationale or logic, a form of activity, which we call 'a game'.

We may extend this notion to other organised activities, each with its own special concepts, ways of thinking and acting, values and aims, its special concepts and *language*. One thinks of the technical jargon of engineering or of a science laboratory, the specialised rules of life, even etiquette, the habits and values of Army officers, or again the highly specialised language of music, with its own entities, values, rules, logic and concepts (the notes of the scale, harmonic relations, pitch, tonality). These can all be called 'games'—each with its 'language game' which people play with language in playing it.

It is particularly interesting that the notion of 'games' has been extended farther still. All these examples are modes of activity or special forms of living; but what about Weber's notion of an ideal type of civilisation, of the rational order of the whole of Western European capitalist *society*, meaning by that not just its economic system? Forms of life, and the language in which ideas, concepts and ways of living are embodied and realised, can be modes of action, or 'games', shared by a whole people of a particular time and culture, and exhibited in all the attitudes and behaviour patterns which make it up. Thus we see the 'game' of modern capitalism as far more than that played in running an economic system with political overtones. Of course (and as Marx himself and Marxists have always recognised), capitalism includes the complete 'social consciousness' of a period of world history. And Dilthey and Rickert, and after them Weber and Parsons, saw this as all part of the 'game'.

Weber was the first deliberately to construct a model, a conceptual system, a paradigm, the actual rules of the game for the capitalist social order. His 'ideal type' gives us a language, the rules, the values of the working of the system, the pattern of its institutions, and its psychology. It covers far more than its economics, as we have already seen. It includes the behaviour patterns and motivations, the organising forms and the political government which enforce the rules of the dominant class which Weber recognises and regards as a necessary part of the social order. In fact we have here, in this form of life, the complete world order which embodies 'the spirit of capitalism'. 'We are born into this order, and for us it appears to be reality. Our minds are wholly conditioned to its 'language games' and modes of thought and behaviour. It constitutes the entire range of our consciousness.

This model is for Weber not arbitrarily constructed as a parlour game might be or a new form of sport; it is the logic, the grammar, of one historical phase of social development. Weber derives it from his observation of our commercial attitude to everything, the fact, in his own words, that 'all our motives are pecuniary'. It is in fact veritably a language *game*—'the money game', 'beggar my neighbour', buy cheap and sell dear, the gamble on the stock exchange, financial take-overs, profitable invest-ment. This is the game operating not only as the mechanism of the business world and the industrial system, but pervading the consciousness of our acquisitive society, and of all classes in that society. As Marx showed long ago, the way of life, the ideology of the ruling section of the community become the mentality of society as a whole.

The ideas of the ruling class are in every epoch the ruling ideas: i.e. a class, which is the ruling material force of society, is at the same time its ruling intellectual force. The class which has the means of material production at its disposal, has control at the same time over the means of mental production, so that thereby, generally speaking, the ideas of those who lack the means of mental production are subject to it. The ruling ideas are nothing more than the ideal expression of the dominant material relationships, the dominant material relationships grasped as ideas; hence of the relationships which make the one class the ruling one, therefore the ideas of its dominance. The individuals composing the ruling class possess among other things consciousness, and therefore think. Insofar, therefore, as they rule as a class and determine the extent and compass of an epoch, it is self-evident that they do this in their whole range, hence, among other things, rule also as thinkers, as producers of ideas, and regulate the production and distribution of the ideas of their age. Thus their ideas are the ruling ideas of the epoch.[3]

The ways of life and the ideas of the ruling class become the ways of life and the ideas of the whole community. There emerges a 'form of life' or 'language' which pervades and dominates not only the economy but all human relations and especially the arts, broadcasting, the cinema and, of course, advertising.

Every game has an objective—to put the ball between the posts, to score runs, to checkmate the king; the money game has its single goal too—to make more money. And Weber is only playing the game when he allows no intrusive values to interfere with it.

The game then has its own values and is constructed and

organised to secure them. It is therefore beside the point to introduce standards or rules from another game, such as the moral principles and ideas which are so often grounds for criticism of the working of capitalism. Weber declares that such principles, often regarded as moral absolutes, are really no more than our subjective or class preferences. The capitalist system itself, he argues, is built on just such preferences, those of the bourgeois class, his own. It is foolish to interpose complaints about inhumanity, injustice and hardship, just as it would be foolish to criticise the play on a football field from the point of view of the values of behaviour off the field—to complain that the centre forward has taken the ball away from his opponent quite roughly and had taken it up the field and planted it in the net, very very much against the wishes of the other side. Nor may you criticise the economic system for pursuing its own ends, those of the business world, by bringing in the rules of a quite different game for the purpose.

This, then, is what Weber means by a value-free sociology, and the economists by a value-free economy. They mean that in the money game, in capitalist society, only the chosen goals on the basis of which the system is built can be allowed to count.

It should, however, be remarked that the insistence that the social order is a self-sufficient activity and that interference from other spheres has no rational ground is really quite groundless. True, the sociologist is here on better ground than with any dualist conception of society. But he fails to see that a challenge to its authority can come from *within* society, from the men playing the game, who don't like it and have devised a better one. After all, why not? The whole of history has been nothing other than a succession of man-created systems, of forms of life. The capitalist game is just the last of these, and can claim no finality. It is not a fact of nature but a transitory human creation. We made it ourselves, as we have made many systems and games before; and are even now in the process of making the next, a project already on the agenda of history.

We shall proceed at once to indicate the nature of Weber's 'ideal type' for our society. It is, of course, the model of a *capitalist* society, in its whole nature, in its aims and in its methods. As Weber sees it, it is the outcome of men acting under a common motivation and finding the appropriate means for attaining their chosen ends. 'That end is *gain* through producing commodities for profit. This seems to Weber to be the value orientation of all reasonable men (speaking from his own experience and the attitude he shares with his class, as he himself makes quite clear). This, then, will be the *meaning* of all that goes on in a society based on this model.'

What next has to be established is how the methods of attaining these ends are to be discovered. This Weber explains in his theory of *adequate causation*.

'Weber recognises that causal laws like those of the physical sciences are only obtained as the result of the repetition under experimental conditions of exactly the same causal sequence. This is impossible in the social sciences, for exactly the same conditions never recur and the same casual sequences are never repeated. The social sciences, therefore, need their own method, which he calls that of 'adequate causation', to obtain the system of objective possibilities which constitute the dependable regularities of society.'

Weber tackles in this way the question of how we find the right causes to attain the ends we seek. He does this by a most ingenious system of hypothetical analysis based on the conviction that it will be sufficient if we can locate the factor which, when removed, would make the decisive difference in a given sequence of events. The presence of this factor may then be accepted as an adequate explanation of the events. A cause is adequate if without it the end desired would not be achieved or the event we want to explain would not happen. Of course there are very many antecedent causes associated in the production of any effect. We want to know which is the essential one.

The only way in which to arrive at a judgement of the causal significance of a factor is to ask what would happen if the factor in question had not been present or had been altered.[4]

To take some examples: If the Austrian Archduke had not been murdered at Sarajevo, would the first world war have taken place? If we believe that in fact it would still have happened, then the murder could not be regarded as an adequate cause of the war. If a person is not stung by an Anopheles mosquito can he get malaria? In fact if we remove this factor, he does not get malaria. Therefore to be so stung is adequate to explain our getting the disease. It is of course not the only cause, but it is an essential factor, since the associated factors or possible causes would not be in themselves sufficient to cause the disease. There is no need in detail to describe what would have happened if the selected factor had not operated; it is enough to know that things would have been different.

It is important to understand that this is not explanation as the calculated *resultant* of the antecedents, as in calculating the stresses and strains in the structure of a bridge, or locating the cause of engine failure in a car; for the necessity we are looking for can only be found by *imagining* the results if the alleged cause were not there. This is the method, and the only method, for explaining unique historical events and for finding the causes of actions involving human behaviour. The result that it gives is not logical certainly, and cannot be, because the causes of human behaviour depend on motivation. As a result, if in an otherwise similar case the motivation is different, the causal result will be different too.

The discovery of scientific laws in physics and chemistry does not proceed in this way. It operates with the idea of the effect as a mathematical function of the cause, giving a calculable resultant. In history and human behaviour, on the other hand, the accent is on the uniqueness of the event because of the multitude of (unrepeatable) coexisting factors, including the motives of the participants, creating a complex of factors which will never again occur. No such event can then be repeated as in a scientific experiment.

The important elements are not here common to all humanity and identical in all cases, in all times and in all places, for value systems are diverse; there is a plurality of different possible systems, so that the same concrete materials will give rise not to one historical result but to as many as there are, in this sense, points of views and values involved. There can be no one universally valid system of general theory in the social sciences. The relativity of value systems introduces an element of relativity into the social sciences which raises in an acute form the question of their claim to objectivity.[5]

Under these circumstances we have to be content with only an 'adequate' cause. In matters of history or social action the best that can be done is to determine with some show of plausibility causes adequate to account for the events and consequences of human actions.

What this does enable us to achieve is a system of general concepts or laws for what goes on in society, as long as we remember that such 'laws' can never possess the same degree of certainty and universality as those which we establish by experimental testing in the laboratory, and that they only hold for societies with the same motivation, with the same 'meaning' or generally accepted goal. Their validity is strictly limited to the values which the causal systems are constructed to secure.

The importance of the 'ideal type' is that it explains a particular complex social situation, that is to say an existing, functioning, ongoing society, in terms of its 'frame of action', its total meaning, its intentions, its actions. This meaning is not given by listing the antecedents of actions or events, because in themselves these could have been used for various purposes. In these cases we know for what purpose, not by examining the antecedents, but by recognising the motivation and the selected end.

No society, no event in history, no pattern of social behaviour can be explained, or can make sense, unless we can express it in a hypothesis, or model, or ideal type, which makes clear the motivation behind all its causal processes. It is that which gives the social phenomenon its *meaning*.

There is no meaning of that sort in any sequence of physical events. There is no *purpose* in nature, as medieval people used to suppose. The sun does not come up because of some benevolent purpose of warming us. The very essence of science is the removal from its causes of purposes, vital forces, intentions. All such thinking is finalism, the teleological approach, which science had to get rid of in order even to get going at all. But in human affairs nothing can be understood except in terms of intention and purpose (with the exception of the mindless actions of the insane or the psychopathic behaviour of the unbalanced). It is purpose and intention that give meaning to human actions and social phenomena, and are therefore necessary objects for social science, for sociology.

Motivation means ends sought because they are valued. Therefore in society every causal sequence, every law system, embodies a value and has no significance apart from it. It has been set up precisely as a means to attain some value. Such laws or rules or generalisations have no validity, *no reason*, in themselves, but only in so far as they secure those values. Thus the economic laws of capitalism are not the laws of nature apart from man, like those of physics, they are not absolute or final. Their validity depends entirely on the particular motivation of the society in which they work and its ends. They are valid for no other society. This then is Weber's understanding of economic law.'J

We can now understand why Rickert and Dilthey rejected the method of the physical sciences for the understanding of society, of culture, of any and every civilisation. No mere description of sequences of cause and effect tells us anything about that. What we want to know is *why* these casual processes have been set up. Thus if we are witnessing a game of football or chess, or looking at the scene on the floor of the stock exchange, or watching a pop music festival, the mere actions as such can be totally meaningless. We want to know *why* people do these things. What is it all about? What are they up to? But this holds not only for a game or some particular activity, but for a whole community, or society, or civilisation. Durkheim and others showed us that to understand a primitive community one must get at its whole spirit, its intentions, its motivations, its life style. This understanding, which, Dilthey and after him Weber called *Verstehen*, is achieved by re-thinking oneself into some past period in history or some unfamiliar community or game or club. One must put oneself in the other people's place, try to experience their objectives and values. It is thus that we create an 'ideal type' for any society or activity that we want to understand. And we do so only in terms of its goals, its values, its motives.

Such an 'understanding', however, is quite barren in itself unless at the same time we grasp how the causal sequences attain the objects set for them by that group. We must see every sequence, every rule of the game as it is actually being played before our eyes, as working for the object of the game and as an expression of its meaning. Thus if you want to understand what chess is all about you need more than a general description of the intention of putting the King in check. One must learn the strictly defined moves of the different pieces, the rules of the game exemplified in the actual gambits in play. If one wants to understand what Association Football is all about, one must know more than that the ball has to be kicked between two posts; one must know the meaning of 'off-side', the special job of the backs, the forwards, the goal-keeper, the complex rules of the game. And one must see all this in operation—the game as a going concern.

Similarly in society, having grasped the basic principle, as explained by Weber, of profit-making as the sole motive of production, of class ownership, of the wage system, of investment, one must see how all these activities take the form of specific economic procedures, laws, economic institutions of capitalist society.

This is why Weber proceeds from *meanings* to *operative laws*. No meaning can be grasped apart from the causal methods of achieving it; and no causal laws have any significance except as operating in terms of the meaning of the whole game. The laws or general pattern of action show how the game goes, how the system works, *what it really is*. We apprehend the motives and designed causal sequences together.

One important corollary follows: The necessary causal laws established to attain the selected ends also establish what Weber calls the 'objective possibilities' of the system or game. Nothing outside these moves or these operations falls within the scope of the settled aim and purpose. You cannot introduce the rules of cricket into football to secure a quicker win. Thus under capitalism you are limited to those laws which secure the aims of those who made the system to achieve *their* values. This establishes the *maximum potential consciousness* of those who have set up the game, or economic system. The laws and rules cover all the objective possibilities. Anything outside these limits is beyond the range of their consciousness, of their comprehension.

This understanding is not of a static system, but of an ongoing process. It is concerned with social activity and practice. Following the recognition of people's intentions, behaviour follows interests as a projected act. On this basis we formulate *types* of action schemes, through which we arrive at sociological concepts of a systematic character.

The concept of action is basic for sociological analysis, and purpose is always in advance of every act. Weber stresses the centrality of intention for all sociological investigation; and it will be realised that this is absent in the investigations of natural science. It is characteristic of human actions that they should be done 'on purpose': that there should be a basis of purpose upon which the structure of the act should be erected and to which it must conform.

The orientation of action naturally involves a wide variety of motives. But the circumstances that along with other causes at least most of those involved are so motivated, defines the model to be binding and increases the probability that the action will in fact conform to it, often to a considerable degree.[6]

It is the fact that there are these regularities of action that makes an interpretative sociology possible.

NOTES

1. Weber, *Objectivity in Social Science*.
2. T. Kuhn, *Revolutions in Science*.
3. K. Marx and F. Engels, *The German Ideology*.
4. Talcott Parsons, *The Structure of Social Action*.
5. Condensed from Talcot Parsons, *The Structure of Social Action*.
6. Weber, *The Theory of Social and Economic Organisation*.

Capitalism: Its Origin and Nature

Weber does not approach capitalism as an economic system, or as the consequence of technological advance and the invention of machinery operated by mechanical power. For him it is essentially a form of civilisation, to be apprehended in its entirety as at one and the same time a culture, an economy, and a value system with its special motivations and its special form of organisation. Towards its making go many factors, all of which play their essential parts in the emergence of the ethos which characterises the life of Western society today.

Of these factors, one was the development of the rational spirit which came to dominate science, law, economics and even religion from the end of the eighteenth century. Another was the simultaneous appearance of the free labourer and the industrialist with his accumulated capital. The labourer was 'free' in the sense that he had no land or other means of subsistence; the accumulation of capital was the result of the mercantile activities of the pre-capitalist world. Finally, there was the Protestant religion which more definitely than any other factor embodied the very essence of the new civilisa-tion—'the spirit of capitalism'.

Weber saw capitalism as the consequence of there being a number of propertied men with money to use, who were possessed by a common spirit which produced a complex of rational modes of profit-making. Its fundamental note is the application of arithmetic to industry—cash accounting, the recognition of the absolute importance of the profit-and-loss account. Weber asserts that this takes on an altogether new importance in industry and business. It is the most important aspect of the new spirit of rationalisation. Capitalism comes to reflect 'economy' in the ordinary sense as saving, as deprivation therefore, and discipline—the ascetic aspect of business activity. This we now see as enforced upon human behaviour, and by nothing more effectively than by the Protestant ethic.

Protestantism marked a radical change in religious thought and feeling. Catholicism laid the emphasis on salvation by the sacramental Grace made available to members of the community of the faithful by the Church, and for them alone; salvation fitted men for heaven; it sought a transcendent other-worldly goal. Protestantism, on the contrary, looked to the right use of the world in the dedicated Christian life, the consecration of our life and our talents to our 'calling'. For the largely middle-class membership of the Protestant churches that calling was our daily duty, in trade and business. A life of systematic hard work became the religious equivalent of a monastic asceticism: abstention from luxury and from the dissipation of our energies in the pleasures of the world, and a life devoted to the calling God has appointed for us.

> We need not bid for cloistered cell
> Our neighbours and our friends farewell.
> The common round, the daily task
> Will furnish all we ought to ask;
> Room to deny ourselves, a road
> To bring us daily nearer God.

So ran the poem which became a well-known hymn among all the Protestant churches of England.

This was only one of the sources of the rationalised life style which created the spirit of capitalism. It was not its sole or even a sufficient cause but, in Weber's words, 'an element which, were it to be theoretically excluded, would have resulted in a very different result'. Aron makes the position very clear:

Weber selected the characteristics which seemed to him peculiar to Western capitalism. Protestantism is not *the* cause but one of the causes of certain aspects of capitalism.[1]

This essential element is the idea of fulfilling one's life in one's occupational calling. Economic activity is consecrated, and seen as having a spiritual value:

To serve the present age my calling to pursue.
O, may it all my powers engage to do my Master's will

Rationalisation is the fundamental principle in Weber's scheme of things and the essential part of his value-orientation. Reason is almost, if not quite, a value in itself. One could say that when men began to apply reason unimpeded by religious authority, magic, spiritual forces and predetermined ends, not only did science come into existence but the modern world appeared—the capitalist world.

This conception of a law of increasing rationality as a fundamental generalisation about systems of action . . . is then the most fundamental principle that arises from Weber's work.[2]

The fate of our times, Weber believed, is characterised by rationalisation and intellectualisation. This means that there are no mysterious or incalculable forces that come into play, but man can master all things by reason and calculation.

Capitalism is present wherever the industrial provision for the needs of the group is carried out by the method of enterprise, irrespective of what need is involved. More specifically, rational capitalistic establishment is one with capital accounting, that is, an establishment which determines its income-yielding power by calculation according to the method of modern *book-keeping and the striking of a balance.*[3]

Weber's pious reverence for the ledger makes it the sacred book of the religion of making money. When one first reads the above passage the sudden descent from the sublime to the banal comes with a slight shock—"book-keeping and the striking of a balance"![1]

Elsewhere he again stresses that the capitalist system rests on "the expectation of gain by the utilisation of opportunities for chances of profit and therefore implies a purely pecuniary involvement with work".

What next emerges is the notion of *class*. Capitalism involves a clear distinction between the property-owning 'acquisition' class and the property-less working class. The owning class has secured "the opportunity for the exploitation of services on the market", control over the means of production, capital funds, and marketable commodities. It exercises monopoly advantages (*a*) for the possibility of investment, and (*b*) in the sale of economic goods and the purchase of expensive goods for the monopolists—in other words, a monopoly of the ownership and control of the productive enterprises of the system.[4] The capitalist system requires, at the same time, the separation of the workers from the means of production in order to secure their labour under conditions profitable to the employer and which reserve to him the direction of the enterprises.[5] Wages are kept at the minimum by the hunger motive, for the workers must labour for what they can get and "they run the risk both for themselves and their personal dependants, such as children and wives, of going without their food", if they do not accept these conditions.[6] This great advantage to the employer depends on the labourer being 'free', that is to say relieved of his dependence on his own plot of land and the possibility of working at his own craft with his own tools.

Finally, the separation of the worker from the means of his own subsistence is the guarantee of the necessary discipline in the factory, based on the rationality of individual control by the administrative grades and the rational domination of the workers.

Weber sees capitalism as essentially a form of *domination* "as an objective and inescapable technological law". The context of Weber's analysis is precisely the age of rationalisation, which decrees that economic rationality requires rational domination—domination at almost any price. Capitalism thus becomes, in Weber's terms, the mathematicised, technological *domination* of men.

The dependence of the material fate of the masses on the continuous correct functioning of the increasingly bureaucratically organised capitalist machine, the pressure steadily intensifying until the thought of the possibility of their deliverance from it becomes ever more utopian.[7]

Weber denies the right of anyone to interpose with the claims of humanity in this process. And he does so, not because of his ill-nature or hardness of heart, but because, in the first place, he regards all *values* as the subjective choices of individuals. There is no philosophical justification for an absolute, universal moral law as such, or for the natural rights of man. This is not to say that there are no values. Of course there are; for the whole of social life is the organisation of man's activities in the pursuit of such values; and that is exactly what capitalism is. But having thus *chosen* your values, that is to say, your attainment-goal, it is *this* value that takes precedence as far as the methods found necessary for reaching it are concerned; *their* value justification lies in the fact that they are the means necessary to secure ones own values. By what right can extraneous moral principles be allowed to interfere? In whose interest? In that of the workers? But they are members of a society whose common interest is secured by the efficient operation of the economy. No utopian, idealistic moralising can, from outside the system, based on appeals to some abstract moral ideal, have the slightest validity, any more than a sensitive mother's protest when her child is hurt by having a tooth stopped. What is rationally necessary to achieve the chosen ideal is the sole moral criterion and court of appeal. This is what is meant by a 'value-free' economy. It means free from interference by illegitimate outside moralising in the value-controlled and value-oriented economic process. As Weber declares:

In such matters the whole understanding of the fact is halted where a scientific scholar permits the intrusion of his own value judgements. [8]

Science abhors value judgements. If we are to be rational and use the only appropriate means to attain our valued end, we must renounce all philosophies and all ethical criteria which interfere with the rational means to that end. These must never be allowed to influence us in making our decisions. Of course we accept the values that we ourselves have chosen, but these are *built into the model* and do not operate from outside the economic process. Weber, therefore, accepts the ethics of responsibility, as he describes it, which judges the means appropriate for the attainment of its own values by a rational estimation of the consequences rather than by the ethical standards of abstract moral principles.

One of the most important of Weber's theoretical studies was directed to the nature of *bureaucracy* as the inevitable outcome of a rationally organised economy. It arises as the correlative of rationalisation, whether in capitalism or socialism. It is based on the following principles:

(1) The appointment of specific spheres of competence, defined by regulations so that offices are clearly apportioned as are the powers of decision for each office.

(2) Every official is protected in his office and secure in his job so long as he carries out his appointed duties.

(3) The system is a hierarchy with each officer in authority over those below him and subordinate to his own superior.

(4) The right of the superior to regulate the work of his subordinates.

Weber must not be supposed to welcome the incidental harshness of domination either in the working of economic law or by the bureaucracy. They are the inevitable concomitants of rationalisation. We are inescapably involved in the organised system required by capitalism, and we are under its rule.

In conjunction with the lifeless machine the bureaucratic organisation is at work erecting the prison house of that future bondage into which men in their impotence will inevitably be forced, like the fellaheen of Ancient Egypt.[9]

Subjugation to technology becomes subjugation to control as such: technical rationality becomes first bureaucratic control and then political control, and all such control is not additional or external to the system but intrinsic to its construction as a social project.

In it is projected what society and its ruling interests decide to make of men and things. Such an 'aim' of domination is material to the form of technical reason itself.[10]

Weber wrote an important essay on *The Forms of Imperative Co-ordination*. Since his whole system moves increasingly in the direction of the extension of rational economy into bureaucracy and bureaucracy into domination, and since this means the imposition of the severest economic discipline on the 'free' labourer, it obviously requires the support of the civil government, and the question arises as to the consent of the governed to such rule. Such a harsh system of demands cannot expect spontaneous assent arising from the general agreement of society. How, therefore, do we secure the attitude of acceptance? How is it that the *legitimacy* of government is fully recognised?

Weber finds three 'ideal types' of legitimacy operating. As 'ideal types' they do not, however, correspond exactly to any given forms of government or administration. In most actual cases legitimacy will contain elements from all three. The three types are, then: (*a*) the authority of *tradition*, resting on the sanctity of institutions and their representation, which themselves rest on the experience of our predecessors; (*b*), the authority of the totality of established *legal and rational regulations* which secure efficiency in the working of the economy—'the iron force of a network of purely instrumental legal rules'; and, (*c*), the non-rational, emotional recognition accorded to leaders of exceptional power, a self-guaranteeing *charisma* such as we find in the great religions and likewise with military leaders, good and bad.

These are all types of legitimate domination, and Weber believes that no stable society exists in which obedience does not rest on at least one of these forms of acceptance—and it may rest on a combination of all three. Domination is essentially *non-coercive*. There is a normative consensus. As a correlative of this we shall certainly find that ruling classes secure their own position of authority by special methods of persecution to establish the legitimacy of their domination; and, in the words of Wright Mills, that may well mean that among such methods none is more effective than "the power to manage and manipulate the consent of men".[11]

Weber had no belief at all in democratic government and saw 'the will of the people' as pure fiction, psychologically invoked by propaganda or charismatic leadership. There must be élitist rule. The people are incapable of judging issues. If the development of technology and administration moves in the direction of political democracy, that democracy must be *managed*. This is the place for the full utilisation of the charismatic popular leader in what Weber called '*plebisciary democracy*'. Parliamentary machinery requires the popular leader to maintain his charismatic authority at all costs, at the price of losing his job. Here the party, the machine, and the demagogue play important roles in taking over the actual control, first of the mass movement and then of parliament. It is the party bosses who articulate the political issues with a view to securing popular support. Henceforth the people can only choose between charismatic leaders, for it is only this type of leader who can rally the masses by his magnetism and emotional appeal and establish effective domination. The legitimacy of this form of government, while formally derived from the will of the governed, is in fact derived from the ability to govern of the representative of a political machine through which the real economic dictatorship operates. The Party organisation finally gains consent for its policies in an election won by its "power to manage and manipulate the consent of men". Weber calls this process *Führerdemokratie*.[12]

The above is no mere commentator's gloss or biased interpretation of Weber. It does not interpret but rather transcribes in as concise a way as possible the theories expounded in his *Zum Begriff der plebiszitären Führerdemokratie* and other political treatises. Nor should it be supposed that Weber himself took a grim satisfaction in his account of the development of capitalist society and its apparently bureaucratic and political dictatorship. On the contrary, he was deeply pained at this development, but he saw it as the necessary consequence, the logical unfolding of the value-free capitalism which he had described and analysed with the strictest objectivity in accordance with his own doctrine of ethical neutrality. That the outcome should meet with ethical disapproval would not be unexpected but would be totally irrelevant.

It is clear that Weber repeats many of Marx's judgements on capitalism, and takes a far more candid and realistic view of it than most economists and sociologists. His theory has been called a bourgeois derivative of Marxism, but in two essential matters it misses what Marx was getting at. In the first place, capitalism is not seen historically as a late phase in the transformation by man of his world, his society, and himself, through his own activity in satisfying his needs and creating new ones. In the second place, and for a similar reason, Weber fails to see that capitalism has itself created the conditions for its own supersession—that by its own economic achievements, which have taken the economy beyond the scarcity which was the original basis of the capitalist economy, it has rendered necessary and possible the transcendence of its 'ideal type', of its model. By missing the historical perspective Weber is locked in his own 'ideal type' of society; he sees it as something permanent, with all its harshness, and experiences increasing disenchantment in its later period of frustration and obstruction.

Nevertheless Weber goes beyond the simplistic empiricism which can get no farther than the observable mechanism of capitalism. Whereas Durkheim and the structuralists could only see the system as an existing working mechanism, in much the same way that we see the tides and the movements of the sun, moon and stars, Weber sees the system as the manifestation of 'the spirit of capitalism', that is to say, as the rational expression of any economy that is based upon private ownership and the profit system as the natural source of investment capital. He has found the driving force, the originating principle, and he has shown how its effective working requires a mechanism of exploitation and a system of domination to support it, and how the whole system creates alienation and disintegrates the human personality. What he misses altogether, besides the historical perspective, is the inevitability of internal crisis and disequilibrium, although this was clearly seen, not only by Marx and Engels, but also by Rosa Luxemburg in her *Capitalist Accumulation*, and also by Hobson and Hilferding. Weber sees no fundamental inability of the system to continue indefinitely on its course of accumulation, exploitation and profit-controlled expansion.

As we briefly review his 'ideal type' and its creation, we must again draw attention to the fact that it is not, and never was intended to be, a *theory* derived from and verified by the economic data of modern society. It was an imaginatively devised *model*, imposed on the facts to make sense of them; and, as Weber himself says, unlike a hypothesis, which being an inference from the facts is susceptible to continuous modification to bring it in line with the facts, the ideal type is incapable by its very nature of modification. If certain facts turn out to be inconsistent with the model, and he admits that they certainly do, there is nothing, he declares, that can be done about it. A considerable range of inconsistencies and shortcomings are quite inevitable when working with a model of this sort. You must just put up with them as long as you keep the model.

And the necessity of the model is that it is the logical expression—and the only logical expression—of the basic presupposition of the economy as a member of capitalist society sees things. Weber frames his model, as he himself says, on the basis of the values and desired ends developed as his own attitude towards life, as a man acting in the world of reality. This attitude was, and in his case had to be, that of a member of the upper class of the German bourgeoisie. It remains the attitude today of the bourgeoisie of every land, and of those members of society who derive their ideas from their ruling class.

In so far as they rule as a class and determine the extent and compass of the epoch, it is self-evident that they rule also the thinkers, as producers of ideas. Thus their ideas are the ruling ideas of the epoch.[13]

The theory of capitalism derives not from the observation of natural phenomena, but from the values and aims of a class that sees the economy as designed to serve its own interests primarily and only secondarily and as a by-product the interests of society and of the labourers.

It is precisely that sort of society that capitalism really is. And its logical implications have by no one, except Marx, been better developed in all their harshness, ruthlessness and alienating consequences, than by Max Weber.

We pass directly to the inner despair of Max Weber as it pours into his later works, his profound sense of 'the disenchanted world'. This world, empirically observed, was indeed for him, a detestable place and 'a house of bondage'.

NOTES

1. R. Aron, *German Sociology*.
2. Talcott Parsons, *The Structure of Social Actions*.
3. Weber, *General Economic History*.
4. Weber, *Theory of Social and Economic Organisation*, in Eldridge.
5. Weber, *General Economic History*.
6. Weber, *Wirtschaft und Gesellschaft*.
7. Ibid.
8. Weber, *Wissenschaft und Beruf*.

9. Weber, *Gesammelte Politische Schriften*, Munich 1921.
10. H. Marcuse, *Industrialisation and Capitalism in Max Weber*.
11. C. Wright Mills, *The Sociological Imagination*.
12. For a detailed analysis of Weber's concept of 'leader democracy,' see Mommsen's *Kölner Zeitschrift für Soziologie*, vol. 15, and the chapter on 'The Concept of Plebiscitary Democracy', in Mommsen's *The Age of Bureaucracy: Perspectives in the Political Sociology of Max Weber*, from which the above account is taken.
13. K. Marx and F. Engels, *The German Ideology*.

7

The House of Bondage

The quality that characterises the whole of Western civilisation and modern industrialism in its capitalist form is *rationalisation*, the term which Weber uses to describe the human condition that it has brought into being:

The fact of our times—says Weber—is characterised by rationalisation and intellectualisation, and above all by the disenchantment of the world. . . . There are no mysterious incalculable forces that come into play, but rather do we master all things by calculation. This means that the world is disenchanted.[1]

The world has become increasingly an artefact governed much as one controls a machine. This is associated firstly with the ascendency of technology, and secondly with bureaucracy. Reality, declares Weber, has in consequence become dreary, flattened, utilitarian, leaving a great void in the soul of men. This must be faced with all the courage we can muster, for it is our inevitable fate as the children of the Age of Reason.

Weber makes the philosophical point that we have never actually *found the world to be rational*. Through our own thought-forms, by means of which we interpret it, by our ideal types, we have *imposed* a rational pattern on reality. But the thing in itself we never comprehend or even touch, it remains a chaos of the disorganised and fragmental reality in which reason makes no inroads. In fact, as rationalisation increases, the irrational gains in intensity.

This is the key to Weber's thought; it dominates his entire philosophy. Man succeeds in rationalising the relationships comprised in his 'type' of organised system, but nothing else. These he controls, and he can assert their scope and effect, but beyond their narrow and artificial scope life and the world remain fundamentally irrational.

We see this also on the level of a pluralism of values, and indeed, of other possible social models or systems. Since all values are subjective, empirically life is a chaos. There is not the slightest reason why *one's own* intuition of the good should square with the values which the capitalist economy manifests and which dominate our whole life and society. There is no possibility of harmonising economics, poetry, morality and art. No harmony exists between power, need, interest and knowledge. If you choose one you reject the others.

The spheres of value are not only independent of each other but are in irreconcilable conflict. If we leave aside the war of ideals and return to the field of social ethics, we come to the opposition which dominates the whole of Weber's philosophy of action: the opposition of the two ethics of *conviction and responsibility.* If we disregard circumstances and question only our conscience it convicts us of inhumanity in our social practice; but if we take our necessary assumptions into account, that is to say the goal whose values are to determine all our actions, and the necessary means to reach it, then *that* ethical position overrides that of the intuitive opposition of conscience. If one is a sociologist and claims to set forth objectively the action-frame of society one must submit to the relentless commands of the chosen situation and reject the claims of the moral sense altogether. This is what Weber means by 'ethical neutrality'.

There is, however, a remarkable example of irrationality appearing *within* the ideal type-created society, not alongside its rationality, and opposing it, but as its effect. For the operation of the *formal rationality* of the system brings into existence what Weber calls *substantive irrationality*. There is, therefore, he says, 'an unavoidable element of irrationality in economic systems'.[2] For instance, 'it is not wants as such but effective demand for utilities which regulate the production of goods by profit-making enterprises'.[3] Therefore marketable goods may appear on the market but not enough of those required to satisfy human needs, either because they are not the most profitable to produce and sell, or because there is not sufficient purchasing power among those who need them. In England today the economy produces houses of the £20,000 to £30,000 kind, but not the lower-priced houses which the working class purchaser can afford either to buy or to rent and not houses in sufficient numbers for renting at a reasonable figure. This is what Weber describes as *substantive irrationality*.

This is the kind of thing that Weber himself noted as already a common feature of the capitalist economy. But irrationality can take a far more devastating form. The steady carrying forward of entirely rational processes, strictly according to economic law, even in Weber's time, but even more so beyond it, creates disastrous effects. The recurrent economic crises which culminated in the Great Depression of 1929 to 1933 reduced world trade by two-thirds, closed mines, blast furnaces and steel works. Coal output dropped until 1,000 pits were closed. Production declined by 50 per cent. The production per head of Britain's whole population dropped to £34. Extreme measures were taken to restore prices to a level which could make it possible to restart the factories by destroying the unsaleable surplus. Immense quantities of wheat, coffee and other commodities were destroyed in a starving world. In U.S.A., Roosevelt secured in 1933 the destruction of 10,000,000 acres of cotton.

Yet all this was considered irremediable and un-preventable. Its causes were the entirely *rational* laws of the economy, its effects *substantive irrationality*.[4] Very few recognised the insanity, the sheer irrationality of it, or asked, as one critic did: "Would a maggot starve because the apple was too big?"

There is surely a theoretical problem of great significance here which demands the search for its basic cause and origin. Reason is realised in capitalism as the historical task of the bourgeoisie. Behind the value-free technology and its economic organisation lies the initial value-orientation which Weber recognises, that is, the accepted interests of the men who built a system directed to a given purpose. Weber identifies the purpose as industrial enterprise for private gain and the satisfaction of needs by the purchasing power of wages, wages being strictly dependent upon the profitability of the concerns in question.[5]

On this basis a number of necessary consequences follow, which Weber carefully notes, and which we have already indicated in the terms of his own analysis. The economic system works rationally only under the conditions which experience and reason find indis-pensable and which therefore constitute the necessary limitations of our existence under capitalism. The regulation, discipline, freedom of the worker to become a wage-earner (freed from land and from means of production of his own); the pressure of the need for capital accumulation; the strict accounting system with its profit-and-loss balance; the pressure of starvation compelling men to take the wage required by profitability—all of these Weber shows in detail, point by point, as the essential conditions of capitalism. They make up his description of how the system must work.

The inner logic of Weber's capitalism, however, is *not* that of an autonomous system. Its efficiency is not for its own sake; it follows from what determines its attainment goal from outside. It is neutral or value-free only in the sense that nothing must interfere with the rational means to the chosen goal.

Even its rationality, the rationality of capitalist technology and production is severely limited. There is a great deal that capitalist production is not allowed to do. It cannot build houses, it cannot rationally satisfy human needs, or raise wages to the amount necessary to absorb potential output. Therefore what happens is that under the value-choice of its end which Weber declares to be, like all value-choices, completely arbitrary, *rationality becomes irrational*. It was the outside orientation by bourgeois interests, by the bourgeois choice of its motivation and goal, 'that developed the substantial irrationality of capitalist society that appears on every side.

What is important is that the rationality that is only rational as the method to attain an end, now becomes accepted as reason itself, as though it had no outside determination. Thus the means to this end become the end in itself, and *irrationality becomes reason!*

Thus the value-free economy by its own working leads to a criticism of its working, and its own concealed value-orientation. It manifests its own criticism. It develops the criticism of its valuation, and of the rational operation by what it does to men. Inhumanity is included in the rationality of its final balance sheet.

How the bureaucracy and its political support and enforcement through plebiscitary democracy gets its way by 'the power to manage and manipulate the consent of men' we have already seen, and how all the agencies of domination are relentlessly at work, as Weber says, 'erecting the prison house of bondage into which men in their impotence are forced'.[6]

It is here that Weber's analysis changes to self-criticism.

"Was there irony in Weber's concept of reason, the irony of understanding and disavowal? Is he perhaps saying: is *that* what you call reason?''[7]

Max Weber did not contemplate his age of reason with equanimity or with the cheerful complacency of so many subsequent British and American sociologists and economists, but with a sardonic acceptance of the inevitable. If you are a Machiavellian you do not wring your hands because you can't make omelettes without breaking eggs. If you are a Nietzschean you do not contemplate the ruthlessness of the master race to 'lesser breeds without the law' with anguish. These things are not pleasant, but let that be a lesson to the sentimentalist who, it seems, will never realise the irrelevance of his moralising.

In Weber's world view rationalisation meant a 'scientific' view of man in society, and that, for him, means an evolutionary acceptance of the struggle for existence. This is the Darwinian component that goes so obviously with the Nietzschean emphasis of Weber's argument. "There is no peace in the economic struggle for existence. Only those who take the appearance of peace for the truth can believe that the future holds peace and enjoyment of life for our descendants."[8]

This exposition is not an indignant commentary on a position that in Weber's own mind and writings envisages an optimistic, or at least an acceptable picture of human life quite neutral in its judgements. On the contrary, Weber is clear and explicit in his harsh, despairing judgement of the outcome of what he describes as a value-oriented mechanism, the objective and necessary means for the attainment of its goals. What he sees, what is involved, he steels his soul to accept as inevitable, making no attempt to disguise its nature.

The essential fact of social life for Weber was the Hobbesian war of all against all which reaches its climax under the economic conditions of capitalism. Weber vigorously argued that no one should deceive himself as to the inevitability of that struggle, or comfort himself with the illusion that a social order could be devised in which recourse to conflict could be lessened. Nor would this warfare be confined within the nation, it must necessarily be *between* the nations. A candid look at reality must not, for a moment, hope "that there might be any other way than the fierce struggle of man against man... It is not peace and happiness that we shall have to hand over to our descendants, but rather, the principle of eternal struggle for survival and the higher breed of our national species.... There is no peace in the economic struggle for existence.... Those of us who, in comparative comfort, owe their lives to the waging of that same loveless, pitiless struggle for existence in which not millions but hundreds of millions decline and waste away in body and soul, year in, year out, or lead an existence which is without any kind of recognisable 'meaning' must learn to accept this as inevitable."[9]

We have referred earlier to the venerable figure of Tönnies who realised clearly that contemporary capitalism with its loss of community had entered a period of systematic decay of sociality, and to George Simmel, friend and brilliant colleague of Weber, whose image of *Metropolis* saw in our society the destruction of individual autonomy and dignity in the face of overwhelming social forces. These men were scholars of wide erudition and established reputations who held no radical views and were not engaged in problem-solving, but simply reacting to the world about them. They had no theory as to why things were so. What they said was not the conclusion of a philosophy of society as it was with Weber, but perhaps their pessimism is even more persuasive from this very fact. For them this was the unexplained, but indisputable nature of capitalist society, and there was nothing to be done about it. Their considered view was that in the capitalist world man suffered 'alienation', by which they meant a profound malaise, a feeling of impending disaster, a sense of spiritual exhaustion, or, as others see it, a feeling of being abandoned, forgotten, caught up in the purposeless stream of life, left rudderless, on its tempestuous seas.

Marx saw such alienation arising because all economic and commercial relations had been transformed from personal relationships into impersonal operations of the market. In the purchase of men's labour, the man was purchased with it and became a mere tool or instrument for other people's ends, a commodity, a thing. Human individuality becomes at once a commercial object and man is estranged even from himself as well as from other men. Thus the social forms of capitalism have become antagonistic to a true society and to the self-achievement of the individual.[10]

It is remarkable how close Weber came to all this as the nemesis of capitalist rationalism when he says that:

Precisely the ultimate and most sublime values have retreated from public life, either into the transcendental realm of the mystic life or into the brotherliness of direct personal relations.[11]

Without sentimentality, Weber, Simmel, Tönnies and Marx saw the relentless transformation of European civilisation into one based increasingly upon impersonality. In Weber's words:

It is horrible to think that the world will one day be filled with nothing but these little cogs, little men clinging to little jobs, and striving towards the bigger ones. . . It is enough to drive one to despair. It is as if we were deliberately to become men who need 'order' and nothing but order, who become nervous and cowardly if for one moment this order wavers, and helpless if they are torn away from their total incorporation in it.[12]

What conclusion does Weber draw as to our attitude to this destiny?

To the person who cannot bear the fate of the times like a man one must say: may he rather return silently to the bosom of the Church. After all, they do not make it too hard for him. . . . Integrity, however, compels us to state that for the many who today tarry for the new prophets and saviours, nothing is to be gained by this yearning. We shall meet 'the demands of the day', in our vocation. Let each find and obey the demon who holds the fibres of his very life. Not summer's bloom lies ahead of us, but rather, the Polar night of icy darkness and hardness.[13]

It might be thought that, fortunately, things are not anything like this now—consoled by the assurances of Daniel Bell that the end of ideologies, that is, of socialist criticism of society, has arrived, and that government control of the economy has overcome the remaining intractable areas of capitalism. But today it has become very hard indeed to reconcile any such picture of events with the reality, when the most serious economic crisis since 1931 is looming up.

As to the disappearance of poverty and other hardships in our Welfare State, the complacent must be singularly restricted in their reading on this topic, when the books and journals of the experts on the endless question of the stability of our economy confess their desperation at the insoluble problems of the economy. The facts show, without question, an *increase* in the poverty of the submerged tenth, and a worse housing situation than at any time in recent history.

If Max Weber were alive today his judgement would be as little blinded by complacency and optimism as it was in the eighteen-nineties and the second decade of this century. Now, as then, he would pray in the face of such complacency to be delivered "from all the easy speeches that comfort cruel men".

NOTES

1. 'Science as a Vocation', in *From Max Weber*.
2. Weber, *The Theory of Social and Economic Organisations*.
3. Ibid.
4. Ibid.
5. Weber, *General Economic Theory*.
6. Weber, *Gesammelte Politische Schriften*.
7. H. Marcuse, *Industrialisation and Capitalism in Max Weber*.
8. Weber, *Gesammelte Politische Schriften*.
9. Ibid.
10. K. Marx, *Economic and Philosophical Manuscripts of 1844*.
11. Weber, *Politics as Vocation*.
12. *Max Weber and German Politics*, ed. J. P. Meyer.
13. Weber, *Essays* (slightly abridged).

Talcott Parsons and Systems Theory

It is certainly the case that, chronologically, Talcott Parsons succeeds Weber, but in the development of sociological theory he directly follows Durkheim. What he essentially did was to enlarge and systematise the structure of Durkheim's organic society, to explain more completely the conformity of individual actions to the requirements of the system, which his predecessor had left as cheerful assumptions of inevitable compatibility, whereas in fact such conformity is highly problematic. Parsons became, therefore, the exponent of classical structural functionalism.

Functionalism proposes a model of society conceptualized as a system of social relationships and institutions organized into an ordered and self-maintaining entity by a common pattern of norms and values, which ensures both the reciprocal interdependence of its parts and the consequent integration of the whole.[1]

This is essentially a biological analogy for the separate parts each of which performs functions required by all the other parts, and above all by the whole for its continued existence. If one functioning unit goes wrong all the rest and the organism itself perish—the heart or the kidney in the human organism furnish examples. It is precisely in connection with his own model of society that Parsons raises the problem ignored by Durkheim: the potential tension between the units of action (individuals) and the demands of the system; indeed he considers *the question of order* and its maintenance as the crucial issue in functional theory.

How, then, is this order achieved and maintained? Firstly, in relation to *the environment*: this is the question of the economy and is a simple problem of adaptation. Secondly, we face the problem of *the activities of individuals* and the legitimacy of rule and discipline. Thirdly, there is *the problem of deviance*, of the unsocialised individual who does not keep in step.

Putting aside the economic issue, which is not our present business, we come, then, to the adjustment of the actions of people in society as a growing concern. This requires, firstly, a *goal* for the whole system to which all the units contribute, and then the *integration* which maintains co-operation between the individuals in pursuit of this goal. This is secured by an ordering or controlling mechanism which must have the consent of the governed.

We come next to the question of how everyone is to be kept in line. This does not happen automatically. It is primarily a question of *motivation*. According to Durkheim, the individual is directed by the collective conscience which creates and constructs his personal moral sense. But how this happens is precisely the problem which Durkheim does not attempt to answer. The question, then, which Parsons has to answer is how to

create technically effective methods by which the ends approved by the co-operation may be achieved and of maintaining efficient co-operation between them.[2]

Talcott Parsons proceeds to show that the social system

comes into existence in the structural and functional form required for this purpose, and is created by its interacting processes. Every individual must of course play his proper part in this complex organisation, and so the crux of the matter is how this is effected—as between one person and another. One person's goals must not clash with anyone else's. Everyone must from the first take account of everyone else. Each must be led to *accept* and to *expect* just what aims he may seek and just what limits he must conform to. There thus emerges *a norm of expectations and of limits for every one*, each conforming to the expectations of the others.

This implies a background of socially standardised roles and meanings shared and accepted by everybody.

This raises the possibility of dilemmas that have to be overcome—one can imagine the possible conflicts that are bound to arise unless one slides over the problem by assuming that it is obvious that everybody's good is secured by conformity and so no problem arises. But is not this the same problem that Durkheim evaded? It has simply turned up again at a later stage and in more precise terms. It has not been solved.

Talcott Parsons sees an emergent network of social relationships, organised and balanced to achieve the common goal, which exactly standardises all the different roles. Each individual person has both his own role and his own aim, and is the person with whose actions those of everyone else has to harmonise. Veritably we are in our very nature social individuals if we are geared and conditioned and educated and motivated like that! As Parsons so well says:

This view contrasts sharply with our notion of society as being composed of concrete human individuals.[3]

How is the miracle worked? He explains that every individual role must fulfil the standardised norms and values laid down for it, and will be articulated into the system through processes of *education* and *external control*. Parsons calls the first process the *internalisation of roles*, so that everyone expects precisely what he should and knows his limits. The second process is the control of deviance by socially devised mechanisms of *external* control.

The reader has probably by this time realised that the argument is moving in a circle, that which had to be proved is really assumed before the process of explication has even begun. By the time we reach the 'internalisation of roles' we must feel that we are being sold something the exact nature of which cannot unfortunately be divulged.

At the beginning we are told that the real problem is that of *order* and it is this that we are going to hear about; but then we are told that the nature of the system itself is such that interdependence in the relations of the components creates the unity and order of the system. But if the system itself is *defined* in terms of its order how can it be that the problem it sets out to solve is that of order?

⌐Parsons then goes on to show that determination of action does not come from without but is *within* the constructed system, for the system itself arises out of the activity of the components. The norms and roles and limits appear in virtue of their recognition and acceptance by the persons concerned and *thus* constitute the system. The structure and its rules is thus a function of the acting individuals themselves, the internalised role-expectations, neatly balanced by each person being trained to expect every other to play his part. All the sets of expectations thus interlock to produce a pattern of standardised behaviour.⌐

This looks terribly like a colony of rats after emergence from a Skinner Box, all their reactions conditioned to perfect reciprocity to achieve the will of the conditioner.

The problem of deviance which Parsons finally raises rather painfully bears this out. But it is difficult to see how it could even arise. He suggests, however, that the values of an in-group might conflict with the overriding out-group. But how this deviance in the sub-group arises is itself a problem, if the society is so integrated by centralised values that all its expectations are standardised.

The more one contemplates the issue the more one comes to the conclusion that the conception of standardised expectations assumes precisely what has to be explained.

The mistake too often made in philosophical and sociological discussions is to regard a concept belonging to a system of thought or explanatory theory as though it were itself a fact, something *concrete*. It is the assumption that we have reached finality and touched reality when in fact we have only constructed another set of explanatory concepts or useful models. If we say, let us treat heat as a fluid and then we can speak of it flowing from a high level to a lower just as water does, we must not make the mistake of assuming that heat *is* a fluid. It is a useful model only so long as we don't do that. To do so is to reify the concept. It is what has been called 'the fallacy of misplaced concreteness'.

Every step in the empiricist account of reality takes the object as described *in terms of a particular viewpoint and in the language of the corresponding concepts* to be reality. But every such account of things turns out not to be a final explanation. Things are not so. Concepts useful for a time become problematic, to be dissolved by a new set of concepts upon a new level.

Durkheim's theory of society was not by any means a final explanation. It required the elaborate analyses of Talcott Parsons, who produced his intricate system of roles, expectations, and functional units labelled Goal-Integration-Attainment-Maintenance and so forth. Clearly, more than any system hitherto advanced, Talcott Parsons' is the most complex series of abstractions within abstraction, going on indefinitely without ever touching reality. But it seeks to convince us that these abstractions *are* the ultimate reality we are looking for. Not at all. This is the very acme of misplaced concreteness; we have not moved an inch nearer reality. Parsons has only re-stated the problem several times removed so as positively to hypnotise the inquirer into the belief that here, if he could only believe it, is the truth at last.

The most obvious form of misplaced concreteness is simply the error of treating the social system as a biological organism when in every basic respect it is not like that. Society constantly reorganises itself. The biological organism is amazingly stable in a form determined by the set of gene patterns handed down through millions of generations with a minimum of variation. If the organism falls into malfunction it perishes. In a society it reconstructs its order.

Societies are characterised by continuous change of their structure. Far from conforming to Talcott Parsons' type, society varies and has in history varied in the most astonishingly diverse patterns and regularised itself in as many different ways.

But Parsons has no use for change. He declares that

A general theory of the process of change of social systems is not possible in the present state of knowledge.

Clearly he reifies *one possible model*, excluding its modification, and excluding the possibility of seeing the type he has in mind as merely one very recent system bearing today few signs of stability or permanence.

We cannot but conclude that in the whole of this exposition we have never really got off the ground. We started with the taken-for-granted common-sense view of the social world as objective reality, and when it grew problematic we did not really analyse it, we only translated it first into the concepts of functional society, like that of an ant-heap or a native tribe which had not developed beyond the overwhelming consciousness of tribal unity. This, however, was as problematic as the naïve descriptions offered by common sense. We then constructed an elaborate model of all possible interactions, describing the same static everyday world and showing how it maintained its equilibrium, and was so organised that it could not and would not ever change.

But this, too, is only the incorporation of the features of our common-sense world into a set of high-level formal deductive propositions concerning a reified social system which disguises its own banality in its organisational complexity. The whole model takes for granted what it sets out to explain—not only social order, but how, in history, society came into existence, how it has changed from period to period, how today it is still in process of change.

Perhaps we shall be accused of favouring a metaphysical theory of evolutionary development. We are doing nothing of the sort. We are looking for entirely concrete beginnings and processes which archaeology, in its reconstruction of primitive society in the stone age and thereafter, knows quite a lot about, theories based on impeccable evidence. We are looking for the stages in pre-history leading up to the ancient civilisations of the New East, Egypt and India. After that we shall examine the changes in recorded history. This is not evolutionary metaphysics, it is history and pre-history, and it is strictly evidential.

What structural functionalism lacks is just the sense of history, or, indeed, any interest at all in history. It remains stuck in the immediate present. It makes the passing moment the model of society as such, it erects a formal model of a passing phase of history as the paradigm of society in all its changing forms and forbids any movement from the existing state of affairs by ruling out social change as "beyond the scope of social science".

Fortunately sociology, before this retreat into the reification of the *status quo* which ended in a static formalism opened up a new vista: a philosophy of history which saw social systems conforming to no one fixed type, but demonstrating the creative power of the human spirit. It was a theory with its own difficulties, but it marked a complete break with both the sociology of utilitarian individualism, as it appeared with the economists, and the petrification of the existing form of society by the formalists.

It was from the group of new thinkers in the University of Heidelberg, Windelband, Rickert, Lask and Simmel, that two remarkable men appeared to attempt the recreation of sociology. One of these was Max Weber and the other George Lukacs.

NOTES

1. David Walsh, *New Direction in Sociological Theory*.
2. Walsh, loc. cit.
3. Talcott Parsons, *Societies: Evolutionary and Comparative Perspectives*.

9

Conflict and Class

A really extraordinary feature of Weber's sociology, in view of the fact that the law of 'domination' appears as objective technocractic law and that society is, therefore, for the non-owning working class, in his own words, 'a house of bondage', is that there is so unquestionable an acceptance of this state of affairs. Significantly, however, Weber shows us that such acceptance is only obtained by a plebiscitary democracy based on 'the management and manipulation of the consent of men'.

Weber does not, like his disciples and exponents in contemporary sociology, ignore class antagonism or reduce it to 'status envy'. He is emphatic that rationalisation means a division into the controlling, owning class, motivated solely by profit, and the working non-owning class, forced to accept its lot under the threat of starvation.[1] But in Weber's world no one resists or even protests.

Weber lived in the industrial country with the largest and best organised Marxist political party in the world. He knew the *Communist Manifesto* and *Capital* very well; the conflict with Marxism is implicit in all he wrote, but the issue is never the possibility of the revolt of the masses. Was revolution so menacing that he felt unable to think about it, or was he conscious of it but unwilling to discuss it?

Sociologists have often failed altogether to notice class conflict, or when they have discerned it have argued, like L. Coser in his *Functions of Social Conflict* (1956), that it does 'not contradict the basic assumptions' of orthodox sociology. And they argue in this connection that opportunity for grumbling is a safeguard against disruption and is useful because conflict has its teeth drawn and is domesticated by 'institutionalising' unrest, that is to say by allowing innocuous forms of protest—the hope of all who want 'peace in industry'.

Dahrendorf, in *Class and Class Conflict in an Industrial Society* (1959), does at least realise that the basis of conflict is between those possessing authority and those who are ruled. But he sees this as a conflict appearing in any kind of association from a tennis club to a trade union, and as no more than rank-and-file revolt against whatever clique has collared the committee. Has he joined the ranks of the wishers-away of class conflict?[2]

For Parsons, 'deviance' is a case of psychological maladjustment which must be overcome either by 'internalisation' (conditioning) or coercion. This is now a very common approach by sociologists to problems of conflict. It assumes, for example, that protest and non-acceptance of subservience, domination and exploitation are due to a 'father-complex', thus invoking the Freudian notion that the sons are always conspiring to overthrow the father and gain possession of the mother; or, if not due to a complex of this kind, then it is simply a case of resistance to the right and normal obligations of social living. It *must be* a mental or moral abnormality, because we cannot allow ourselves to believe that there could possibly be *justification* for rebellion. König, professor of sociology at the Universities of Zurich and Cologne, *defines* sociology as 'the process of the social auto-domestication of humanity'.[3] For him the essential problem of sociology is the adaptation of individuals to society. W. Mitze, in Germany,[4] explains that there is no genuine reason for protest and conflict because the plight of the proletariat is not the result of the economic situation but a problem of psychological attitude allied to adolescent resistance to paternal authority. Discontent is not against real grievances or real poverty, and a healthy psychological attitude would remove it at once—there are no rational grounds for it.

Of course, for the structural functionalists, like Radcliffe-Brown and Parsons, anything which disturbs the automatic self-regulation of the interlocking parts of the mechanism is fatal and cannot therefore be allowed. By definition, the social organism *must* resist change. Like homeostasis in the body, each self-regulating function controlling heart, kidneys, liver, blood is essential for life. If any fails, the organism dies. Therefore, all sociologies which accept the existing system as *given*, as something which must be taken for granted in the way we have to take the laws of mechanics, physics and physiology for granted, postulate equilibrium, or its speedy restoration if disturbed, as the necessary condition of the continued existence of society.

Any contradiction of the basic assumptions of capitalist society, pointing to radical reorganisation on different principles, is out of the question. What alone is tolerable are conflicts of the safety-valve type which can be quickly corrected, as they are corrected in the body by its autonomic mechanisms.

At least one recent non-Marxist writer on sociology, John Rex,[5] has, however, seen conflict not as concerning sporadic cases of minor grievance which common sense and a little give and take could adjust, but as *basic conflict* over access to the means of life, denied to the great majority. There is conflict, then, between owners and non-owners; and with this goes the conflict over political power. Rex seems to think that this is a separate question from that of economic domination, but Weber clearly shows that even under the mask of democracy political power is invariably that of class economic privilege—that is, of those who own and control the means of production. Weber makes this abundantly clear and his arguments have not been challenged even by his modern disciples.

Rex does, however, recognise the possibility of conflict between groups with opposing interests, especially economic interests, where 'one of the two conflict groups dominate the society'. In this situation the ruling class 'would claim that its property system and the power that supports it are the legitimate institutions of society', whereas the opposing group would deny this claim to legitimacy and mobilise power 'to resist the political power of the ruling class' and the myths and ideologies which defend it, and would seek to set up their own standard of legitimacy. 'The most extreme form of the subject group in revolt would actually be engaged in the overthrow of the social system of the ruling class.'[6]

We recall the question of 'legitimacy', and Weber's circular argument to the effect that the acceptance of 'imperative co-ordination' is a necessary consequence of a rational social order. The order is its own legitimation! All that we can usefully discuss, therefore, are the *various forms* that the inevitable, unavoidable and necessary submission takes. Challenge of legitimacy for Weber is *impossible*. On his assumption that only *one* rational economy is conceivable, which is the technocratic system working through its apparatus of privilege, class-ownership and domination, there can be no such dichotomy. Rex, on the contrary, declares that if society is founded on a dichotomy of fundamental interests, there *will* be such a challenge. But even then, he fails to locate the revolution in anything more than rebellion, protest, dissatisfaction on the one hand, and the belief, based only on hope, that the exploited class can offer an equalitarian alternative in the form of 'utopian socialism'.

In consequence his discussion tails off into the hypothetical and the contingent, to questions of quality of leadership, compromise between classes, gaining concessions. Yet suddenly he envisages the possibility that perhaps the subject class cannot make gains commensurate with its new power, 'unless it destroys the basis of the old conflict situation altogether'. But this possibility is not more fully discussed.

We come to the question of change. All forms of functionalism are logically debarred from being able to put forward any sociological theory of change. 'This', John Rex explains, 'is because the whole functionalist effort is devoted to showing why things are as they are. They are as they are because they are demanded by the needs of the social structure.' And of course that there can only be one form of rational society, a functional one, in which every part and its functioning, and every element and person playing its necessary role in that functioning, is interdependent with every other, so that its particular aims, expectations and activity *must* gear in with those of everybody else.

This may be attained in several ways:

(1) By determinism as in Durkheim, where the individual is no more than the expression of the whole.

(2) By internalisation, that is to say educating and conditioning the individual to do his duty and restrict his ambitions, 'in that state of life to which it has pleased God to call him'.

(3) By 'the rational processes of a technocratic society' operating through bureaucracy and domination on the basis of consent secured by manipulation of the sentiments of the subject group.

(4) By totalitarian dictatorship in the interests of the owning and ruling class which overturns the democratic process and ensures that it will never return. This is a process of unconcealed coercion and not discussed by Weber.

It has to be noticed that there is no difference in principle between any of these ways of obtaining submission.

Efforts have been made to replace Weber's plain statement of the basic economic separation of ownership and work with a discussion of 'class' which obscures the basic fact with a consideration only of *status*; dealing with such questions as 'U' and 'non-U' speech habits, keeping up with the Joneses, working-class approximation to middle class standards, as in Lloyd Warner's fascinating study of the Six Classes of Yankee City—Upper-upper, Lower-upper, Upper-middle, Lower-middle, Upper-lower and Lower-lower—by which time we shall have forgotten about Weber's analysis of capitalist society, a result perhaps from some points of view eminently desirable.

It is clear from Weber's analysis that class-consciousness and class conflict are not created by subversive propaganda. They are built into the structure of society and represent the plain recognition of one's fate in it. Weber discusses all this again under the heading "the chances of life". In Weber's rational society "those who are disadvantaged by it are made lowly by necessity in accord with reason". Class is a reflection in society of the working of "the quantitative rationality of the market". It is made manifest by *who gets what* and *who does what* in a capitalist society; what people *get* and *do* depends on their 'life chances'. These are the expectations, probabilistically estimated, of length and quality of life. Social class is a function of the general estimation of life chances as good or ill, as invidious or as conferring prestige in the rational system of capitalism.[7]

If anyone is inclined to think that in the Welfare State of our time everyone gets a fair 'chance of life', an extract from an article in *The Times* by its leading columnist may occasion second thoughts.

The fact must be faced that Britain still has a large, insecure, underprivileged labour force, whose pay and weekly budget often mean little more than a hand to mouth existence. These men—and women—do not feel that there is anything particularly enduring about the new found affluence that some of them have found. Relatively few have a secure and regular income. . . . They still feel that educational opportunities are scandalously limited. Society appears to them to be unequal, selfish and irresponsible.[8]

In this context social change would seem not only desirable, but necessary if the consensus required by Durkheim and Weber and Parsons is to be maintained. But radical change is precisely what the model of organism or equilibrium precludes.

NOTES

1. Weber, *Wissenschaft und Gesellschaft*.
2. R. Dahrendorf, *Class and Conflict in Industrial Society*, 1969.
3. R. König, *Soziologie Heute*.
4. W. Mitze, in *Soziale Welt*, Review of the Association of Social Research Institutes, Dortmund, 1950.
5. J. Rex, *Key Problems of Sociological Theory*.
6. F. Engels, *Socialism, Utopian and Scientific*.
7. D. MacRae, *Weber* (Fontana Modern Masters).
8. *The Times*, January 27, 1961.

10

The Dimension of History

The task of the historian, said Ranke in 1830, "is simply to show how it really was" (*wie es eigentlich gewesen ist*). Three generations of historians have made it their watchword. It fitted perfectly the empiricist tradition, which dominated British philosophy from John Locke to Bertrand Russell, that direct inspection of the 'facts' give us indubitable knowledge.

This theory has, however, been steadily eroded in the physical sciences, in psychology and in philosophy. Naïve realism is based on thinking in so casual and haphazard a way that it is hardly thinking at all. Without taking the least trouble, anyone can claim that his own first-hand experience proves to him that this 'realistic' theory of knowledge is obviously true.

But nature is a *process*, not a collection of separate events. In physics you cannot separate what matter is from what it does. It does not consist of inert particles, but of 'something going on'; perhaps a constellation of electrons in a moving pattern. The individuality of the hydrogen atom depends not even on the arrangement of its electrons, but on their rhythmical *movements*. Within a given instant of time the atom possesses no qualities at all. It only possesses them in a tract of time long enough for the rhythm of the movement to establish itself, just as a dance requires the completion of a series of movements to be that particular dance, which, like the atom, finds only in the completed movement its individuality, its unique reality. Life is the same. The living organism is a continuous process, its being consisting of its past, present and future, taken not in isolation but as a whole. A fertilised egg is not comprehended in what can be said about it histologically and microscopically *at the moment*. We shall not know what it *is* until it has been incubated and has completed its development. There are entities which are only known historically, not as bare existents, but as a *becoming*. This is manifestly so with every passing phase of the history of society, which not only encapsulates its past but is not completely known apart from what it is to become. Here, however, we are not on the plane of things which change because of their own inner dynamic, but of the interaction of men with the social environment, with the historical conditions in which they find themselves. The plane of man's own creative intelligence and action. History is not therefore a predetermined sequence, like astronomical events or the development of an egg, since it depends on men's understanding of their conditions, on their choices, on their decisions. History is man's creation, man's direction of events, and above all of his *redirection*, his capacity *to change the course* of history.

The reluctance of many historians to accept this point of view may be due to the fear of any future which might radically alter the existing state of affairs. To the man so immersed in the *status quo* as to be part of it, in mind, in values, in expectation, in habits, any change of pattern, of conceptual form, spells chaos and disaster. That is why historians in an age of change like ours cling to the present. This is historical empiricism. Yet "the essence of life is to be found in the frustrations of established order".[1] Thought is hampered by the presupposition of the static forms. It is because the timid defender of the present construes the coming epoch only in terms of the forms of order of his own world and his own mind that he sees change as mere confusion.

Slow drift is accepted. But when for human experience fundamental change arrives, human nature passes into hysteria. Then while for some heaven dawns, for others hell yawns open.[2]

Little wonder that, determined to accept the immediate experience of present fact as all we have to go upon, the historian's description of reality is profoundly pessimistic.

This century has witnessed the brilliant conquest of the most distant frontiers of historical knowledge, yet fewer and fewer historians believe that their art has any social purpose, any function as a co-ordinator of human endeavour or human thought. They appear to belong to that dangerous and dying section of western European culture, which had led them to ignore the one aspect of the human story which both makes sense of it and also gives grounds for the hopes of men—that is the material progress of mankind which has gone on from civilisation to civilisation, from society to society, and from place to place, but so far has only paused and never ceased. . . . By progress we mean man's increasing control over the environment, which is historically verifiable. This has rendered more more and more of men's lives longer, healthier, more secure and more leisured. . . . To ignore the implication of the concept of progress seems to me to lead to disintegration and nihilism. In doing so historians turn their back on their social function.[3]

If history is seen as man's mastery of nature by the discoveries of science and the advance of technology from the stone axe to agricultural chemistry and the nuclear reactor, it will be seen also as the creation, stage by stage, of the systems of co-operative work and organisation necessary for the efficient working of each technological stage. By such forms of human co-operation and patterns of human relationships man not only satisfies his material needs but at the same time develops upon them as a basis his cultural life, and enlarges the whole world of his values, aesthetic, intellectual and social. Yet at every stage, the more successfully organised a society is, the greater the expansion and efficiency of its methods of control both in production and in securing the health and welfare of its members. In each great period of revolutionary change, the expanded and more efficient methods, and especially the discovery of new sources of power, render obsolete the types of organisation which were appropriate to the earlier stages of inventions and industrial methods. The *pattern* of organisation has to be changed.

Marx and Weber in the nineteenth century both described the totally new type of social organisation that had to be created to operate machine industry. It was more than a new economy. The whole of human culture was revolutionised, the business world replaced the landed gentry and the old-fashioned city merchant. That was what interested Weber, and it was also the concern of Marx. It was the richness of human life, its humanity, its culture, its philosophy, its art, which took on new forms in the industrial age.

Capitalism, for Weber, created a new kind of man, a man with new objectives, new values, new habits, a new type of personality and no ideals except those of business success. In Marx's terms (though, of course, no simple one to one relationship is suggested here):

In acquiring new productive forces men change their mode of production, and in changing their mode of production, their manner of gaining a living, they change all their social relations. The windmill gives you society with the feudal lord; the steam mill society with the industrial capitalist.[4]

Nor is culture the mere epiphenomenon of which the economy is the reality. No conception could be more stunted than this crude reductionism which was detested as much by Marx as by Weber. Because we cannot have any culture unless we can keep alive, that is not to reduce culture to mutton chops. But it is peculiarly true that since the 'capitalist spirit' is so very much an affair of calculated profitability, the whole of capitalist culture, more than any previous form of life, is permeated by its commercialism and its dualism between the life of privileged mastery and of exploited labour. The feudal lord rejoiced in the songs of the troubadour and the cathedral of Chartres. The sacred book of the businessman, Weber tells us seriously and earnestly, is his ledger, and his temple is the Joint Stock Bank in Main Street.

The essential thing about Marxism was its clear awareness of change, of the obsolescence that overtakes every technical method and, in turn, every way of organising the labour to operate it. Marx, unlike Weber, sees capitalism not as *one* permanent form with no future, but as developing through three periods:

(*a*) First comes the period of its rise as a progressive form of economy, guided and inspired by that 'spirit of capitalism' which Weber attributed to Protestantism, but which had its ideological roots in so much more—in Adam Smith, in Tocqueville, in Bentham, in the individualism of Leibniz, and the rationalism of Diderot.

(*b*) Then follows the period of its establishment—of a prosperous, stable and expanding capitalism. That was the age known to Weber.

(*c*) Then follows the period of its decline owing to its inability to utilise to the full and for all mankind the potential productivity that it had created. This period is one of anomalies, frustration, increasing internal conflict and international rivalry. If it is not resolved by development to an economic form appropriate to the potentialities, capitalism enters a period of self-destruction and the paralysis of its powers.

Each of these periods produces its own philosophy, its own ideology, the expression of its inner spirit. First the ideology of belief in *progress*, then of the *stability* of the system, and finally that of capitalism in decline—the one that we know so well, reflected in our literature and poetry, in our drama and the film—the age of *anxiety*.

Where anomalies appear in scientific theory the scientist does not write pessimistic poetry or take to drugs; *he reconstructs his theory*. This may well be not a modification but a total change of model, an extension beyond the limits of the *reason* operating at the previous level. The social scientist is in very much the same position. He knows perfectly well that medieval thought operated within limits which had to be transcended when the Renaissance dawned; and that the Renaissance ideological world was itself transformed with the coming of the mercantile world of trade, and then again by the commercial world of investment capitalism. But there is an important difference between the ideological changes in society and revolutions in scientific theory. For science it is the same world, but seen in new perspective, in a totally new way, that of modern physics, of evolution, of new theories of matter, of genetics, of molecular biology, of the post-Newtonian theories of Einstein. But for the social scientist his new world is *not* the same. His own theories, those of capitalism and individualism, *have themselves changed the world*, and this is what has made his concepts, his point of view, his presuppositions, obsolete.

In 1968, at the time of the student troubles, someone chalked up on the walls of a Cambridge College: "Do not adjust your mind—there is a fault in reality." Well, not a *fault* in reality, for what has happened is that capitalism as a creative force has driven reality forward until it has gone beyond the model, the theory, beyond Weber's 'ideal type'. This is the moment when change is indicated by the condition of affairs in which the limit for expansion and for the utilisation of potential production has been reached, and in consequence serious anomalies and contradictions have appeared in the economy. As Marx says:

The productive forces themselves press forward with increasing force to put an end to the contradictions, to rid themselves of their character of capital; to the active recognition of their character as social productive forces.[5]

In the early nineteenth century we looked for the features in contemporary capitalism which were moving towards the 'ideal type'. In the time of Marx and Weber we found in society *the existing historical model* of capitalism. In the second half of the twentieth century the structures and functions of society *have moved beyond the model.*

The model cannot ultimately exist as an historical reality. Since all historical reality is always in a process of becoming, the model is either a criterion for a reality developing towards it, or, if adequacy between model and reality is maximised, internal circumstances have given rise to a reality that has overtaken the model and moved farther and farther away from it.[6]

At this stage the 'ideal type' of Weber can no longer serve as an adequate explication of the mode of production. Historical reality has transcended the capitalist model and is approaching a new formulation. This is what Thomas Kuhn, describing *Revolutions in Science*, calls a 'paradigm shift'; not a *modification* of theory, but a complete reconstruction of the model, of its concepts, its laws, its presupposition, which transcend its former limits.

At this point it enters a new world *as* thought, and a new

world *of* thought. When a society is shaken by a great elemental crisis, it is in such terms that we need to think. Individuals and whole social classes are pushed and pulled out of their accustomed ruts, forced to confront unprecedented situations, to think previously unthinkable thoughts. In such circumstances behaviour patterns cannot and do not conform to expectations established in ordinary times. The hopeless are fired with hope, the inactive are driven to action, pent up frustrations *burst* forth and enormous stores of energy are released. Time-honoured prejudices and taboos are forgotten. For a while the normal process of social life disintegrate, authority loses its legitimacy, and even the near future is shorn of predictability. These are the characteristics of a revolutionary situation.

It is here that Weber is completely at a loss. When under the inspiration of his 'ideal type' we enter not the promised land but the 'house of bondage', he is simply nonplussed, for his thought is necessarily limited by its own *conceptual form*. We have to remember that Weber is a Kantian. He declares that we cannot know reality, but only the *form* or *model* which we ourselves have constructed, through which alone we know it. But we are dealing with capitalism both as a theoretical model and as an historical reality in process of change. Therefore we are quite able, if we do not allow ourselves to be imprisoned in such a model, to understand and take active part in the actual development of society beyond this stage. For Weber, the capitalist model is only a category of explanation of the unknowable. But we do not see society as if we were examining it from outside, Kantian fashion. *We* are aware of *our* situation. *We* are *within* society, and a *part* of society, and have always been so, as men, as the makers of our society. In the past *we* transformed and made capitalism, and we can transform it again. As Marx said, man is not the mere creature of circumstances, he himself made the circumstances which now press in upon him, and he can make them again as he made them in the first instance.[7] We are the builders of our own history and we do so every time humanity moves forward by going beyond its present form.

The philosophical error into which Weber fell, and other social scientists and philosophers too, is to separate the conceptual system from reality and so give it an independent existence of its own. As an *idea*, it cannot change. It is men who change their ideas, in order to change the world; and thinking is never simply a *reflection* of reality if it is to be effective, but is *critical* of reality, finding ways to change things by getting a better understanding of the actual situation. In just the same way medicine gets a better idea of sickness by means of the germ theory of disease. It is not the original idea of 'disease' that itself evolves into the germ theory. Quite the contrary, the old idea has to be totally discarded.

We have therefore to be on our guard against ever taking for granted the conceptual model for reality. It is when we do so that we miss the historical dimension, as Durkheim does, and Talcott Parsons, and all the empiricists and functionalists. Their thinking, following Weber's, does not envisage the possibility, the necessity of conceptual change; but "systems of thought which are constitutionally unable to take account of change are worthless, and in time of crisis dangerous".[8]

Since Weber has never come in sight of a self-changing world, that is a world in which men are both the makers of history and of themselves, his model of the *status quo*, if it dominates our thinking and is the conceptual form in which we do all our thinking, becomes an ideological bulwark of capitalism. It is not for Weber (as it is for us, if we pause to consider) simply an idea *about* capitalism. *It is the capitalist consciousness* about the world and mankind—and for him it is unalterable, for it *is* reality itself (for us).

To the question of consciousness, the imprisonment of the mind in its capitalist, seemingly permanent 'form of life', we shall return in a later chapter; but there is something more to say on the 'formalism' of sociological dogma.

Philosophy has to escape both from the intransigence of mere fact and from the tyranny of the pure conceptual model which reflects it. This is, in both forms, *reified thinking*. If thought is no more than a reflection or copy of reality, clearly it can never change it. Simple 'reflection' theories either resign themselves to accepting 'the God of things as they are', or invent animistic theories of a society changing automatically, after Bergson and the Life Force theories. Hegel saw history changing because the immanent Idea was unfolding within it. A vulgar Marxism, but never Marx himself who repudiated this Hegelian mysticism, sometimes sees history as unfolding by its own inner laws independently of man. This is pure superstition. Thought to be effective and to move the world must not simply *reflect* reality, it must *understand* it. It must no longer look down from a higher plane on men and things and their history, but become *the awareness and the driving force of action by which man transforms both things and himself and makes his own history*.

Reality is never reducible to, or understood by, a conceptual system separated from its object which takes on an independence and permanence of its own. This is the paralysing *structuralist* conception of theory. Man and his possibilities are then confined to the system which produces him and in which he lives and acts, now raised to the level of an 'ideal type' or a sociology of the world as it is, the future an extrapolation of the present. To escape from the reality tied to our perception by the structural model, we have to place the present in its historical perspective, and see the present as *becoming* and not being, as one transitory phase in man's making of his world, and knowledge as essentially the understanding that sees the necessity for change and makes it.

This is the thought that is no longer the slave to what is

and has to be. It is thought which, working wholly within the *conditions* it faces, creates its own future and does not merely fulfil the destiny fate has appointed for it.

This is to escape from the structural dogmatism by which we establish ourselves in the concept and its immutable principles, complete, finished and un-changeable.

All this would be so obvious as to make argument unnecessary but for the fact that ideological forms are powerful enough to paralyse the power of movement as do poisons in the darts of certain South American Indians. Let us go back to Weber's depressing view of the fate of man under capitalism; it is also the view of Thomas Mann, and Kafka, and Beckett, and T. S. Eliot, and other writers whose art reflects the contemporary dilemma. If the model represents all that there is to know or that can be known, then there are many very good grounds for pessimism, or even for agreeing with Camus that since life has lost its meaning there is no reason why man should not escape in suicide. It all depends on whether we *have* to accept this model of the world. *Is* it final? The empiricists insist that it is, and that only sensational utopianism or irrational mysticism offers any escape—and *that* is illusory.

But *are* these overriding principles and laws, part of the unalterable structure of the universe, or do they have a *social* origin? If we take the former view we will be trapped in the frozen form of the system and helpless before blind fate in the shape of war, unemployment, slumps, despair and neurosis, whirled like a leaf on the gales of uncontrollable economic tempests. And all this anarchy and impotence will continue to be reflected in our culture. But if history as we are called upon to make it offers a forward step, then that shows indeed the objective possibilities and the necessity of change. If we are not hypnotised by present structures and their laws there is a way forward. This possibility we are now to investigate.

NOTES

1. A. N. Whitehead, *Modes of Thought.*
2. Ibid.
3. J. H. Plumb, *The Historian's Dilemma.*
4. K. Marx, *The Poverty of Philosophy.*
5. K. Marx, *Capital,* vol. 3, ch. 27.
6. S. Avineri, *The Social and Political Thought of Karl Marx.*
7. K. Marx, *Theses on Feuerbach,* No. 3.
8. E. Gellner, *Thought and Change.*

11

Evolution and Human Progress

1. THE CONCEPT OF PROGRESS

The idea of progress has characterised western thought since the eighteenth century. Before then the Golden Age was in the past and time had to "run *back* to fetch the Age of Gold". Plato saw all history as the story of social degeneration from government of the wise to democracy, and then lower still to dictaorship by worthless men; while our modern evolutionary approach, whether in its organic form or as Herbert Spencer applied it to society, gives scientific support to belief in progress up an inclined plane: "the ultimate development of the ideal man is as logically certain as any conclusion in which we place implicit faith".[1]

We have never entirely renounced this faith, but in the last decade it has increasingly been called in question, especially by the historians and sociologists. No doubt in the nineteenth century it was too easily construed as an inevitable sequence of events leading to a predetermined goal:

That one far off divine event
To which the whole Creation moves,

as Tennyson describes it. Many saw the historical process as driven and controlled by a 'life force', a teleological principle, which turned what purported to be a rational hope into a metaphysic.

It was this view which Weber repudiated, attributing a materialistic version of it to Marx, though not a single paragraph or sentence in Marx's writings suggests anything of the sort. He repudiated any such view of history. Weber saw all such theories as 'emanative', meaning that the sequence of events is seen as issuing forth in time from some fundamental principle or source, so that everything that appears in history was contained in this *fons et origo*, the later stages being already present in the earlier and thus being the inevitable result of its development.

It is, however, possible to hold evolutionary views both for the organic world and for history without accepting any such metaphysical theory. Biology has established a satisfactory theory of evolution from the origins of life and its primitive forms through the long sequence of plant and animal forms to the highly developed flowering plants and the warm-blooded, viviparous, large-brained mammals, and ultimately man. Contemporary evolutionary biology regards itself as unquestionably describing a *progressive* development, while at the same time its theories are empirical and postulate no 'life force', or teleological principle, or tendency towards a predetermined end. Social evolution has also established empirically the progressive development of society as man's increasing mastery of nature, a theory which can be substantiated by archaeological and anthropological evidence in the pre-historic stages and by historical evidence since.

This is not the emanative theory which Weber, quite rightly, rejects; nor did Marx hold any such metaphysical conception of social evolution. The 'historicist' theory which finds all the future stages already involved from the beginning, to be gradually evolved in the course of history, is not a Marxist view. It was, of course, the Hegelian theory, which saw the end as already there in reality but unseen:

Already fulfilled in truth so that it need not wait for us. Its actual appearance only removing the semblance as if it were not yet performed.[2]

Progress is seen not metaphysically but empirically, on the basis of the evidence that we have for human betterment, man's growing understanding of natural forces, and his capacity to use them for his own advantage. Man has passed in pre-history from the food-gathering and hunting stage to agriculture and cattle herding. He has discovered new sources of energy, from wind and water to coal, oil, electricity, and nuclear fission. He has invented mechanisms of all sorts, from the wheel and the plough to the modern machine. In our times by the application of science to agriculture he has reached the possibility of overcoming the world scarcity of food. In the care of health and the prevention and curing of disease man has made discoveries that have greatly increased the span of human life. Of course there has been regress, stagnation, the self-destruction of civilisations and our own is now facing its crisis; but it is sophistry to ignore the real progress and see everything in terms of the manifest evils of our time, which Marxists are the last to forget.

Progress is not an automatic and inevitable process. It has been won only by intelligence, industry, increasing co-operation in production, and by the courage to go beyond outdated methods, both technical, scientific, and organisational. Yet it can still be questioned on the ground that we have no valid criterion of progress, since our assertion that it is better to be fed than to starve, to be without pain than with it, together with all the evidence that we can adduce for progress, in fact has no objective validity and is based on no more than arbitrary value judgements. It can be argued that what appears later must be better, and that that is our only ground for regarding both biological and social development as progressive. We have confused what *is* with what *ought* to be—the naturalistic fallacy.

There is no progress, it is argued, unless we can find some *outside* standard independent of subjective preference wherewith to decide what is really 'good' or 'better'. Weber is acutely aware of this problem, and surmounts it only by basing his values on his own subjective choice. He does not believe in any possibility of making an ethical judgment the validity of which can be logically established. In ethics he is therefore a 'pluralist'; there can be as many ethical standards, and as many different societies based on these different principles, as you like. Hence the working of his chosen economic system cannot be judged by any general principles of human welfare. There are none.

But of course as far as organic evolution is concerned no biologist judges what he believes to be 'higher' by what has actually survived. He knows perfectly well that evolution concedes survival equally to the *Lingula* brachiopod which established itself 300,000,000 years ago and has not changed, and to man, the latest form of 'progressive' development. He knows also that evolution has produced many regressive types, like parasites, and highly specialised types so adapted to one environment as to be in peril of extinction if it changes. Nevertheless, biologists, without either committing the 'naturalistic fallacy', or making arbitrary subjective judgements, or appealing to absolute transcendental standards, have registered a consensus support, for which adequate reasons are forthcoming, in favour of the reality of biological progress. If we can do the same for society we shall have criteria by which we can judge the claim of Weber's 'value-free' economy, without prostrating ourselves before inevitable processes of history, or appealing to transcendental absolutes, or falling into subjectivity.

We do in fact value our achievements, positively or negatively, by standards that we ourselves have made on the basis of experience, and which have given us enduring satisfaction. No standards are final or absolute. All are open to revision, but many have stood the test of the centuries. For our decisions as to the better, our preferences and choices, we are prepared to give reasons, and we are prepared to criticise them; but we have no intention of being persuaded that there is no basis for our preference for life, health and sustenance rather than death, disease and starvation; or for our conviction that

Life *is* lived 'on a slope', that there is a legitimate demand for sustained improvement based on the belief that this is possible, and somehow human prerogative, and that failure to satisfy this requirement is socially pathological. We do believe in a specific kind of progress, in the possibility of achieving a full and general industrial society, untarnished by remaining slums.[3]

But we do not believe that the total world history is the continuous and inevitable story of a collective and total redemption.

This position enables us to avoid the dilemma of, on the one hand, a metaphysical belief in progress as inevitable, and on the other hand a certain kind of fashionable scepticism; nor are we like Weber compelled to fall back on purely individual prejudices and subjective values —which turn out in the end to be class values, the unexamined presuppositions of a typical member of bourgeois society.

Marxism does not then advance any metaphysical view of social evolution, but sees a significant movement *in history*, often missed, reversed, or denied, but still in one area or another going forward to increase and extend man's control over nature and secure human betterment. Marx ridicules the idea of a general historico-philosophical theory, the supreme virtue of which consists in being super-historical.[4]

Engels laughs at those who want every period in history to be explained in advance without their having to do any historical research. Marx explained that his own work was not intended to cover the whole field of history but amounted to an "historical sketch of the genesis of capitalism in Western Europe". In his *Critique of Political Economy* he mentions the Asiatic, Ancient and Feudal forms of society, but only as indicating in the most general way, and provisionally, social forms corresponding to the different levels of technology, but not suggesting that any one developed into another. There are in fact three or four alternative routes from the earliest stages to the first real examples of civilisation. Marx regards them as so many independent historical formations to be understood in terms of their own categories. That they show a series of advancing technological levels does not mean that all society has moved forward simultaneously in three world-leaps. There is no such linear evolution.[5]

Marx differs fundamentally from Weber in what he holds to be the overriding human purpose and goal of history. For Weber this does not go beyond 'the ideal type' of profit-seeking owning class and the type of society, based on domination, which rationally follows from this motivation. Marx sees the present as a necessary but painful and humiliating stage which creates the necessary conditions for the self-fulfilment of man in the fullness of co-operative relations with his fellows.

When the narrow bourgeois form of society has been peeled away, what is wealth, if not the universality of needs, capacities, enjoyments, productive powers of individuals? What, if not the full development of human control over the forces of nature—those of his own nature as well? What, if not the development of his own creative possibilities, unmeasured by any previously established achievement? What is this, if not a situation where man does not merely reproduce but produces himself in the wholeness of his personality?[26]

II. THE LOGIC OF HISTORY

Weber has no logic of history—only the logic of his artificial model of the economy with its causal sequences based on their causal adequacy, thus giving a Weberian endorsement to empirical economic law. His logic then shows the necessity of domination, bureaucracy and government. As far as its origins are concerned, Weber's logic begins with the principle of rationalism and its gradual spread through Western Europe. His model is framed to give a guiding concept to explain how rationalisation moulds the economic and social system of capitalism.

This is, at any rate, much better than a simple descriptive account of contemporary capitalist society and the usual attempt to deduce its laws in the same way that we deduce the laws of physical nature; but the upshot is not very different, since Weber gives us the economic laws, and also the whole structure of capitalist domination. The empiricist view is reached by illegitimate induction; Weber's system by deduction from the model imposed on the empirical facts. In both, man is seen to be ruled by a law outside himself, beyond his control, authoritative, destructive of his freedom, and threatening his future.

Vulgar Marxism also sees a system independent of man moving by its own logic to the inevitable collapse of capitalism and its replacement by socialism. This is very far from Marx's own position. Marx *has* a logic of history which sees capitalism as certainly real, but not as a natural, unalterable, absolute system like the world of astronomy or physics. On the contrary, it is seen as a highly artificial world, a human construction of institutions and rules and class relationships belonging to a particular phase of history with no more finality about it than the strange world of Ancient Egypt, with its myths of the underworld, its system of priestly rule and divine Pharaohs, as real to the Egyptians as the economic laws are to us, or the medieval period with its domination by the Church and the ideology of scholasticism. These systems were utterly *real*, and yet at the same time *ideological* and passing phenomena. Capitalism is the same, with its laws and institutions, and its ideology.

What Weber takes as the necessary logic of his 'ideal type', of the model of capitalism, Marx takes as a transitory stage in human development. What for Weber is all there is or can be in sociology (on the basis of its presuppositions), Marx sees, historically, and in the light of its decline and transcendence, not as man's inescapable fate, but as most certainly a cruel tyranny, its mechanism not part of the nature of things but an incursion of reality and a system of illusions.

The theme of *Capital*, and especially of the section on *the fetishism of commodities*, is to show that our belief in the final reality of capitalism, of the operation of its impersonal economic laws as a second nature, of the industrial mechanism which man has made but which now controls him, is wholly false, illusory. These belong to what Marx calls 'the illusion of the epoch', representing a transitory stage in social development, a world, indeed, where everything is turned upside down like the image on the film of a camera, in which man has become a commodity that is bought and sold like merchandise and in which human relations have become relations between *things* instead of between persons, in which the process of producing goods for human needs has become a destructive and uncontrollable mechanism.

In his brilliant comparison of the realistic, true picture of his one-man island economy which Robinson Crusoe created, in which everything in the economy is *transparent*, with the capitalist system as we experience it, where everything is opaque, Marx says that these inverted and distorted reflections of the real world will not disappear

until the relations between human beings in their practical everyday life have assumed the aspect of perfectly intelligible and reasonable relations between man and man and between man and nature. The life process of society, this meaning the material process of production, will not lose its veil of mystery until it becomes a process carried on by a free association of producers under their conscious and purposeful control.[7]

This will not take place automatically by the development of the system itself, but, as Marx repeatedly declares, only when the logic of history is seen and understood, only when men themselves tear down the veil and, seeing how things are, take the necessary steps to change them.

III. MAN, MORALS AND SOCIETY

We are now in a position to understand that man can indeed judge his own social system, for it never stood over against him as a natural phenomenon that he simply had to accept, but was always his own creation, both in the past, and now in the form of capitalism. It is only when society and its economic laws are taken to be something observed from without, or imposed upon us as a model for which we are not responsible, that the age-long dichotomy of the economy and human values, ineluctable fact and our rational ideas, what *is* and what *ought* to be the case, appear.

We now see that there is only one world and man as part of it, learning to control nature to satisfy his own needs. He is to that extent the master of his own fate, and not the helpless spectator of an alien reality. We are in this material world engaged in the task of finding how nature works and using its powers for our own benefit. From the Stone Age through history to our own times we have chosen for ourselves what is good *for us*, and there can be no external source asserting the authority of some *good in itself*. What is good must be good for somebody, somewhere, otherwise it is 'good for nothing'. We exercise our own preferences, and we make our own choices; *and* we subject them to criticism and revision, or rejection. It is man's highest prerogative to be his own judge of the validity of his standards and of the rules of social behaviour which he establishes.

With regard to any natural event which we cannot control, there is no moral obligation *within* nature to make it serve human ends. When we use natural means to secure those ends we have to accept the laws of the mechanism and are responsible only for the ends and consequences of the process, in other words we take the consequences of using the means into account, as well as the end in view, when making our decision to use those means. We no longer believe in any direction of natural forces within nature and apart from our utilisation of them, which has an end or a purpose possibly for our good. They are strictly the means *we* adopt for the fulfilment of our own purposes.

When Weber speaks of a value-free economy he treats the rules of the particular model which he has constructed as though they were the laws of nature. (But it must be repeated that since the model was chosen as the rational system to achieve the ends selected by himself, the working of the system is not really value-free, for it serves the ends of the model.) Weber seems to believe that once the model has been chosen we have no alternative but to accept it and the rules of its operation, regardless of the fact that it overrides human values. This is due to the fact that he has no philosophy of history, no understanding of human progress as man's creation, as the utilisation and supersession of a succession of technological stages and the social systems appropriate to them and arising from them. If he saw the situation from that point of view he would see the absurdity of accepting without question means that prove self-destructive. That this course should prove acceptable to Weber, and to many economists and sociologists today, can only be because the economic system in question is one in which the ends of one class are secured by the domination and exploitation of another, and the *ends* are secured by the first class, while the *price* in exploitation and domination is paid by the second. In such a case it is those who benefit who argue that the economy is not to be interfered with for the sake of human welfare, since it is the rational means by which it attains its own ends.

We see at once that the way to overcome this disjunction between value-free means and value ends is to abolish the separation of owning class and working class; and *so abolish their conflicting interests*. If the workers become the owners, then the owners will be concerned with the value control of the realisation of the value aims of the workers. But where an economic mechanism consists not of men but of 'productive units', the whole system becomes reified and impersonal and, as such, destructive.

It is, however, as Weber has most elaborately argued, out of the question that those involved in and subject to his 'ideal type', the capitalist model, should become aware of any *objective possibilities* beyond those involved in and limited by the system's *meaning* for themselves. For them nothing is possible that is not limited by the selected *end*, and by the causal processes logically established as the way to achieve that end. Within the world of this model, all consciousness is limited to those possibilities, and all alternatives must appear *impossible*. So long as this consciousness persists we shall feel compelled to go on with the system whatever its consequences, because, for our way of thinking, beyond 'the game' and its rules there is nothing but anarchy and chaos.

NOTES

1. Herbert Spencer, *Principles of Sociology*.
2. G. W. F. Hegel, *Encyclopaedia*, I, par. 161.
3. E. Gellner, *Words and Things*.
4. K. Marx, *Correspondence*.
5. See E. J. Hobsbawm, introduction to Marx's *Pre-capitalist Economic Formations*.
6. K. Marx, *Pre-capitalist Economic Formations*.
7. K. Marx, *Capital*, vol. 1, ch. 1.

12

Max Weber and Karl Marx

The intellectual milieu of Max Weber was dominated by Marx, and sociology since his day has been increasingly shaped by the need to respond to the Marxist challenge. German scholars took Marx seriously, while in England he was ignored. Werner Sombart, Böhm-Bawerk, Tugan-Baranowski and Hilferding were well aware of the force and scholarship displayed in Marx's *Capital*. Doubtless one reason for their concern was the strength of the German Social Democratic Party, founded and fostered by Marx and Engels themselves, and the feeling that some sort of revolution had to come in a country which was still, at the end of the century, without constitutional government.

Nevertheless, even with *Capital* and the *Manifesto* before him, Weber had not much to go on. He knew nothing of the basic philosophical work of Marx, since revealed by the publication of his neglected and forgotten early manuscripts, which did not begin to appear until 1932. For the most part it was through Kautsky, the theoretician and the leader of the German Social Democrats, that Weber came to understand Marxism, and later through Sombart's *Modern Capitalism*—a scholarly and capable exposition of *Capital*.

In some respects Weber's understanding of capitalism

coincided with that of Marx, though the historical insight was entirely lacking, and Weber took the system as it stood as all there was to know; but they agreed on the primary significance of profitability, on which accumulation for new investment depends; the subsistence wage to secure the maximum surplus for profitable investment: the monopoly of the means of production by one class and its domination of the whole system and its government. Weber understood and defended the 'hunger motive' that kept wages at a minimum and the harshness and impoverishment which diminished the lives of the working class.

Weber's inability to see capitalism as a necessary but transitory stage was due to the fact that nothing was more alien to his empiricist standpoint than a general view of historical development which shows how humanity passes from one stage to the next before arriving at the ultimate stage in socialism. He knew capitalism only as he found it, and lacked the wider view which saw man, over the centuries, mastering his environment and making possible by successive advances a fuller life for mankind. He was unable to grasp this empirically established and by no means metaphysical or teleological theory, and could only conceive Marx's approach in terms of an immanent evolutionary force which swept society forward independently of "the consciousness, the will, and the purpose of man".[1]

This, however, was not Marx's view. On the contrary, he repudiated those who, in his own words:

feel obliged to metamorphose my historical sketch of the genesis of capitalism in Western Europe into an historico-philosophic theory of the general path imposed by fate upon all people. . . . No one will ever arrive by using the master-key of a general historico-philosophical theory, the supreme virtue of which consists in being super-historical.[2]

Metaphysical evolutionism was quite foreign to Marx's insistence on the conscious understanding by the workers of the inner truth of their concrete situation, and their responsibility for its development as the indispensable condition for advance. That this could be regarded as automatic Marx would regard as absurd. Unconscious and automatic development would mean descent into barbarism, only to be prevented by the intervention of "the consciousness, the will, and the purpose of men". For Marx capitalism never 'collapses'. People overthrow and replace it. And the goal is by no means inevitable. For the struggle ends "either in a revolutionary reconstitution of society at large or in the common ruin of the contending classes".[3]

In *Capital* Marx is showing capitalism as an entirely new and unique system of production, an advance on earlier exploitative systems and essentially a new way of organising men in the process of production—the wage system, and a new ruling class who own the monopoly of the means of production. But Marx is concerned to explain that not only is capitalism comparatively newly arrived, but that it is *transient*, creating the possibility and the necessity for an advance to a fundamentally different economy and a more rational and humane way of organising men in production. Change is effected not automatically but when men see how the *successful* development of capitalism outstrips the appropriateness of its own form and enters a phase of dis-equilibrium, which can only be overcome by an advance to a socialist system which breaks the fetters of production imposed by the old economic laws and realises the immense potentialities created by capitalism.

Weber's inability to grasp the conception of phased development was due to his philosophical position, as Marx's developmental approach was also based on a philosophy. Hegel saw history as progressing to greater rationality through successive epochs, each with its distinctive civilisation; but this was a manifestation of the unfolding logic of the Idea. Marx saw the same process, but as the effect of man's creative efforts. Weber as a Kantian had no such historical or developmental perspective. He saw reality as *fixed* by the concepts of the human mind, which knows through the forms of its own inner mental structure. This was the Kantian approach which could not but see reality in terms of its own 'ideal type', so that this became the permanent model of social reality.

Weber expounded his criticism of Marxism in his famous *Address to the Officers of the Imperial Austrian Army)* in 1918. Here he argues that while Marx had predicted an increasing pauperisation of the workers which would lead inevitably to revolution, in fact the prosperity of the workers was steadily increasing. But Marx made no such unconditional prediction. And Lichtheim, himself a consistent critic of Marxism, even went so far as to declare that "pauperism plays no part in the Marxist theory".[4] Marx, Lichtheim says, never expected wages to fall to a point where the entire working class would be at, let alone below, subsistence level. On the contrary, he repeatedly declared that by trade union and political pressure the workers could overcome the *tendency* to depress wages.

Of course, there must be such a tendency because higher wages encroach on profits and thus on the investment which is necessary for capitalism to continue and expand and therefore for steady employment of the working class. But the tendency of wages to fall *could well be reversed.* Marx, throughout his economic writing, made full allowance for countervailing tendencies to the pressure to reduce wages.[5]

Weber is fully aware of the necessity to keep wages down, not because of inhumanity or selfish greed; nor of course did Marx attribute the pressure on wages as due to these causes. Weber puts the economic argument very clearly:

When the limitation of consumption is combined with the release of acquisitive activity, the inevitable result is obvious: accumulation of capital through the compulsion to restrict popular consumption. The restraints imposed upon consumption are for the purpose of making more investment possible, and that, by lessening unemployment, increases consumption.[6]

Weber advanced two further arguments against Marxism in his *Address to the Officers*. The first was that it would increase bureaucracy. But he himself argues that under capitalism bureaucracy must increase both in extent and in harshness. We grant that developed industrialism, whether capitalist or socialist, will be administered by a bureaucracy: but it is the intention of socialists, but not of Weber, to bring it under democratic control by imposing a freely chosen purpose on the industrial system.

This possibility depends upon the democratic populace capable and desirous of determining its needs and making them the guiding principle of the economy and society.[7]

The second argument complained that Marx sought to reduce everything to material motivation, and man was taken to be wholly concerned with personal self-interest and economic gain. This is really too much! Weber himself is the most forthright exponent of *Homo economicus*, and his 'ideal type' is based upon such motivation. As far as Marx is concerned such an interpretation cannot be supported by a single text from any work of his, or from the open book of his own life. Marx attacked both Bentham and Stirner precisely because they conceived man on the pattern of an egoistic and self-centred petty bourgeois shopkeeper—in Weber's own words, as the ideal bourgeois type whose whole existence is determined by calculated gain as measured by the profit and loss of his book-keeping account'. Marx criticises Bentham as "the insipid, pedantic, leather-tongued oracle of the commonplace bourgeois intelligence of the Nineteenth Century". Bentham assumes the shop-keeping petty bourgeois, says Marx, to be the normal man in capitalist society.

But Marx is keenly aware that as long as men are without the basic necessities of living they have no possibility of finding what life is beyond food and shelter. It is therefore right for us, especially in an age of potential plenty, "to arrange the empirical world so that in it man experiences what is really human and becomes aware of himself as a man. . . . Each man must be given social scope for the vital manifestations of his being. If man is shaped by his surroundings his surroundings must be made human."[8]

Is this really 'materialist'? What really fills people with alarm is that if this objective, instead of being left to the benevolent to secure *for* the poor, is taken in hand by the workers themselves, then the frightful prospect of a genuine social democracy appears. This was well put by Lenin writing in 1895 on Frederick Engels:

These people cannot conceive of the workers acting as an independent social force. They look upon the proletariat as a sore and nothing else, and watch with horror the spread of this sore with the growth of industry. The service rendered by Marx and Engels to the working class can be expressed as follows: they taught the working class to know itself, to be conscious of itself and to put science in the place of dreams. . . . The emancipation of the working class is the task of the working class itself.[9]

This does not mean that great political changes are always fought out in terms of class interests as the explicit motive. Marx saw that even the struggle to bring the pattern of social relations into harmony with the new forces of production—a reasonable and unexceptionable motive, one might think—would be fought out in ideological terms, as for instance it was in the struggles against the Popes at the close of the fifteenth century to free rising industrial nations from papal financial exactions and create strong national states. There was no insincerity in men seeing this issue largely in religious terms. The point is that ideological motives of this kind have often been in harmony with the real needs of society. The idea that for an action to be really moral it must be for nobody's good is mistaken and absurd. Marxism is in line with sound ethics when it rejects a sectional aim that is contrary to general interest and supports the policy that secures at one and the same time the interests of the workers and that of the future wellbeing of the country as a whole.

This raises an issue on which there is still discussion: Marx is supposed to argue that ideas play no part in history; that only material and technological forces are effective, and history moves by the unconscious operation of its own laws. This was how Weber interpreted Marxism, and there has been a 'vulgar Marxism' that took this view as well. It was never Marx's position. There is indeed no limit to the misunderstandings and distortions of Marx's ideas, and there is no better example than this one. Weber is supposed to have refuted Marx by attributing the origin of capitalism to 'the Protestant Ethic', a clear example of *the idea* as the originating cause of historical change. But the argument works equally well in either direction; for the urgent need for economic change could be said to *require* new ideas. It is, of course, human intelligence that solves the problems facing men. There is no unconscious force of history to solve them. Marx always insists that change depends on our intelligent recognition of how difficulties are to be overcome. But the difficulty itself cannot give rise to its solution; only intelligence can achieve that.

The real point is to expose the error of separating idea and reality in the old Cartesian manner which persisted from Descartes right through philosophy to the positivism of our own day. What both Hegel and Marx pointed out, and later such thinkers as Whitehead, was that there is only *one* world, and it contains physical objects and events operating under their own laws, and also *thinking* organisms, who discover and use those laws by their own intelligence and for their own ends. *We know* in order to *act*, and by acting we change reality and so know in a different way; and make a new decision in conformity with the situation that we have just brought about. If we want a word for this reciprocal interaction of *knowing* and *reality* we can call it 'dialectical', and there is nothing 'metaphysical' about it.

Thinking, acting and valuing are therefore inseparable. It is foolish to imagine social action taking place like a kettle coming to the boil, as a mere sequence of physical causes and effects in which the 'thought', the 'idea', eventually appears as a mere epiphenomenon, like the whistle of a kettle when it boils. It is equally foolish to think of ideas dropping from heaven, or arising uncaused, or derived from some theoretical system, and then *impinging* upon a material world. What else is our thought at bottom if not the conscious and systematic complement of our social activity? This is what Marx meant when he said that "social existence determines social consciousness". He did not mean that physical being creates consciousness 'as the liver secretes bile', or that it merely reflects it.

Marx and Engels all their lives thought and wrote against crude materialism, and so did Lenin. The whole work of Marx was devoted to changing people's minds, changing their ideas by helping them to understand the actual situation confronting them.

We do not set ourselves oppose the world with a doctrinaire principle, saying: "Here is the truth, kneel down here!" It is out of the world's own principles that we developed for it new principles. We do not say, "Stop your battles, they are stupid". We merely want to show the world what it is fighting about and to express in general terms the meaning of the historical movement going on under our very eyes.[10]

So far from teaching men simply to accept the automatic processes of history, after which their ideas must necessarily follow the material changes, Marx believed that no social progress was possible *unless men's ideas changed first*. "The intellectual victory", said Marx, "must be won *before* we storm the barricades of capitalism."[11]

The aim of Marxism is not, however, to convince people of the truth of a complex system of economic and political theories, but to emancipate them from the blinding and paralysing ideology which holds them in economic bondage—the ideology of Weber's 'ideal type' and its rationalisation. The greatest obstacle to progress is the heavy weight of the systems from which, Engels argued, Marx came to deliver us—the systems of the economists and the empiricists who generalise and form concepts on the basis of *things as they are*, of the formalists who on various grounds create theoretical systems, economic, political or philosophical, and attempt to limit and rule reality by them. No one makes this clearer than Weber with his confessed contradiction between the *formal reason* he is constrained to follow and the *substantial*, the actual, *irrationality* in which it results.[12] And the same absurdity is seen in the economy which declares that we must starve because we have created too much, or which states that the laws of economics show that in a hungry world "an usually good crop can ruin the farmer", and his land must therefore be forced out of production and his surplus destroyed.

When existing 'laws', ways of living, economic rules, political demands, moral obligations, *or scientific theories are* proved inadequate to satisfy our needs or effectively control and utilise our resources, we must call them in question. In science we make a 'paradigm shift' to a new theory; in economics we create a new 'model'; in ethics we frame new rules for social life; in politics we create another form of government. It is *not* rationally obligatory to accept without question an economy that imprisons us in 'a house of bondage' and deprives us of the possibilities of wider living that our resources now make possible.

Society is constituted to make its own rules, and as long as they serve their purpose they are acceptable—but not beyond that moment. When they prove unacceptable and society as constituted does not secure the ends that every society is constructed to secure, then society makes different rules; and such redirection of history is what we mean by progress.

The essence of Marxism is the challenge to the *reification* of the concepts of a transitory and now obsolete historical phase in human development, and to the metaphysical theories which stabilise and perpetuate the concepts of economics and social science, making it appear that such abstract systems rule the world. Marx calls this tyranny of the concepts of the status quo—*ideology*; and he means by that, not illusion, but the absolutising of the once valid concepts of an historical phase, so that their preparation holds up progress, denies emancipation to millions, and threatens all society with decline—the ideology of those whose interests are bound up with the restrictive forms of the present system.

It is this obstruction which prevents the normal transition to new methods of organisation and the consequent widening of liberty, and will do so until the discrepancy becomes so great that society must undergo a violent change or perish.

But the paralysis which the concepts of such types of social and economic structure are responsible for is not simply a *mistake* as to theory; an intellectual blockage; it has clearly a great deal to do with *the range and limitations of the social and political consciousness*, and it is to that question we now turn.

NOTES

1. The phrase was used in a Russian review of *Capital* in 1872, referring to the development of capitalism itself in which men were not conscious of 'making history', though they knew well enough what their immediate purposes were.

2. K. Marx, letter to the editor of *Notes on the Fatherland* (St. Petersburg), 1877.

3. K. Marx and F. Engels, *Manifesto of the Communist Party*.

4. G. Lichtheim, *Marxism*.

5. K. Marx, *Wage Labour and Capital*.

6. Summarised from J. E. T. Eldridge.

7. W. Hannington, *The Accidental Century*.

8. K. Marx and F. Engels. *The Holy Family*.

9. V. I. Lenin, *Frederick Engels*.

10. K. Marx, *Correspondence*, 1823.

11. K. Marx, letter to Eccarius.

12. Weber, *The Theory of Social and Economic Organisation*.

13

Consciousness and Social Change

Weber was one of the first to announce that society cannot be understood in terms of its structure or on the basis of its present factual description. For him every fact, every description of structure, leads back to the *meaning* responsible for it. Even in the physical sciences the 'facts' which are assumed to be immediately given cannot be abstracted from their context and their history. The data which are 'given' embody more than appears on the surface. This is even more obvious in dealing with society. The 'facts' of present social experience represent the present stage of a process that is moving through a sequence of radically different social forms, each with a distinct 'meaning system' of its own to which the individual facts of that system belong, and which gives them their significance. They have no meaning in themselves.

· Each stage in social development, each pattern of society, has therefore a consciousness of its own, 'its own epoch comprehended in thought'. We cannot suppose that in the feudal society of some medieval manorial community people thought and felt, had identical concepts and values and felt in the same way, as the citizens of New York in 1974 or of Tokyo in 1874.

It was the neo-Kantian school of Dilthey, Rickert and

Weber that established the notion of the 'constituting perspective', the *Weltanschauung*, of the historical period or society we propose to study. It is through this lens, and in no other way, that we perceive and know and comprehend any society. The intuitive grasp of the ethos of a society is called its *Verstehen*, meaning its comprehension.

Weber went farther and showed that each perspective is from the standpoint of some special social group responsible for the organisation and ideology of the given society, as the Church was in Europe in the tenth century and the Renaissance princes for the city states of Italy in the thirteenth. The essential feature of Weber's sociology is his emphasis on the value orientation and the corresponding conceptual thought-pattern of the leading class in the society under investigation. It is here that we find the *meaning* of the facts and the *Verstehen* of the system.

Society is thus seen as a totality in which the parts are in reciprocal interaction, a totality not 'given' as a part of *society as such*, but as part of a special pattern of society created by a special group or class, at a particular period in history, from its own unique point of view. Thus each moment or phase or historical epoch has its own 'universe of discourse', range of understanding or conceptual outlook—which is limited strictly to its own world. This constitutes its characteristic consciousness beyond which its members cannot go. Indeed, they will not be able to conceive, in real as compared with fanciful terms, any other mode of life. Such a consciousness—and for Weber and his world it is of course 'the spirit of capitalism'—expresses itself and is limited by what he calls the *objective possibilities* which establish the logic of its thinking, of its aims, of its purpose, and of its behaviour.

From Weber's point of view this would hold for each and every distinct society, each with its own set of concepts, rules, objective possibilities, within its own pattern, like that of the feudal system, or the world of the Church, or a primitive kinship system or of society in Ancient Greece,

Egypt, the Indian caste system or whatever. Within their own ideological limits men will find the necessary meanings to secure the particular ends of their society—the glory of chivalry for the feudal knight, solvency for the modern business man, and very different 'laws' and rules and concepts and structures for different goals.

The substance of Weber's approach is that of his 'ideal type'. This is far more than an economic hypothesis, or a model for capitalist structure. It is *a form of consciousness*—and not in a purely subjective sense, but implying that the *objective* world for our capitalist society, and therefore the only world we know and can know, is constituted and limited by what is objectively possible for rational minds to envisage within its law system—in exactly the same way that in technology and for our objective material world, determined by rigid scientific law, perpetual motion is impossible, water cannot run uphill, every form of physical and chemical activity uses up energy, objects fall according to the law of gravity, high voltage electricity fuses inadequate conductors but is insulated by non-conductors, and so forth.

In the real world a great many things simply cannot happen, the laws of nature cannot be dodged. The same is true for the economic world in which we live, and for our legitimate expectations and our rational projects in society. Our minds are not constituted to envisage what is entirely outside the realm both of *physical* and of *social* possibility. Socially, this means the limits of the basic class structure of our society, which is as inseparable from its economy as the stability of tables and chairs is from the law of gravity. The whole social and human structure of society, as well as its possibilities, its evaluations, how we see people and their actions, is determined by its structure and motivations. In our capitalist society these are the profitability of business enterprises, double-entry book-keeping, the money market, the cash nexus. And in exactly the same way, the reality of the material world, its law of solid objects, its colours, solidity, weight, fragility, toughness, is there and inescapable. In other words, capitalism is not an economic process going on in a neutral world. The capitalist world is as wholly determined in all its parts, all its relationships, all its values, all its motivations, all its class and group stratifications, all its thoughts and feelings, its possibilities and impossibilities, by the spirit of capitalism, as the material aspects are determined by the objective structure and functions and laws of nature.

This establishes the bounds of potential consciousness in the fields of the economics and politics for our society. It marks the limits of what is objectively possible for us. Faced with the grave problems that threaten our society with disaster, neither our economists, of whatever school, nor our political leaders, of whatever party, have been able to find any solution within the limits thus laid down; and any venture beyond those limits appears quite out of the question.

We are in fact experiencing an example of the continuous dissolution of outworn conceptions that always takes place in human thought. It happens with our conceptions of the natural order: gravitation, combustion, the circulation of the blood, the nature of infectious disease; and similarly with our conceptions of society: the 'divine right of kings', the institution of slavery, what classes have the right to vote, the disabilities of women, etc. The overthrow of outdated conceptions is simultaneously a theoretical and a practical matter—the sphericity of the earth was proved theoretically, but also Magellan circumnavigated the globe; political treatises, including a fine one by John Milton, rejected the theory of 'the divine right of kings', but also King Charles lost his head. In our time it is necessary to criticise the absolutism of financial orthodoxy theoretically, but also by actually *doing* what is declared to be impossible.

This is part of the history of man that has consisted in the continuous overthrow of successive forms of thought. As these lose their capacity to serve the economy they become *ideologies* and can no longer claim to be 'laws of nature' or absolutes of any kind. The new position that overthrows capitalism, however, is *not* an ideology—for in declaring that it is both rational and possible to use our technical know-how and available resources for the satisfaction of human needs, it is an unquestionable truth. The countervailing view of contemporary economics and sociology which declares that its *rational* laws lead necessarily to 'substantive *irrationality*' (Weber's term) and actual frustration and misery, *is* an ideology and has to be shown to be so.

This is what Weber meant by the 'objective possibilities', the potential consciousness, the logic of the structure and working of our world strictly limiting what is conceivable for us. The limitation appears in a host of threatening and bewildering *necessities* and impossibilities: mountains of unsaleable butter; cotton crops ploughed in to keep the price up: famine one side of the river, glut the other: wheat burned and people starving. One period sees years of unemployment, closed mines and factories, the mercantile marine laid up to rust at anchor; while at another period it is inflation that threatens disaster. And all this carries with it a sense of inevitability, these things seeming to be part of the chances of life, like the 'plague, pestilence, famine and sudden death' of the Prayer Book. And there is a pitiful, helpless acceptance of it all. As Hindu widows once accepted that they should be burned on their husband's funeral pyres, so today we are supposed to accept disasters which the theorists have announced as a necessary consequence of the formal rationality of the system, as objective as the multiplication table and quadratic equations. The economic side of life constitutes one world of necessity, physics, meteorology, thunderstorms and earthquakes, the other side; both together establishing the total limits both of what can and cannot be done, and of the range and structure of our expectations, and of what cannot be avoided. Everything is as it is, reality is whatever is the case; and we have to take things as we find them.

It is amazing what people *accept* as part of the nature of things, as human destiny, to which to their minds, their consciousness, is completely attuned. "I have been hanging people for years, but I have never had all this fuss before," said Lofty Milton, Rhodesia's executioner on the occasion of protests against the execution of black dissidents.

It was the intention of Marx to demonstrate in *Capital* how such irrational happenings, how forces destructive of personality, arise as the spin-off from the mechanisation of human relations when men's labour and men themselves become market commodities. Then the whole productive system, which man himself has made, becomes his enemy, while as long as there is steam in the engine and the wheels revolve, its inexorable laws grind on, and

Nor all your piety and wit
Shall lure it back to cancel half a line.
Nor all your tears wash out a word of it.

The entities, laws and concepts of this world have become concrete *things*. Human relationships, entered into to let men live, become relations between economic factors—things. We are hedged in by man-created forces: impersonal, uncontrollable—a second nature, like natural reality, existing from all eternity, outside man and independent of him, and yet to our dismay, created by ourselves.

Recent discussions on the methods of scientific discovery have been concerned with the significance of revolutions in fundamental theory such as, for example, the change from the Ptolemaic astronomy for which the Earth was the centre of the universe, to the Copernican system which saw the Earth and the other planets revolving around the sun, or more recently, Darwin's evolutionary hypothesis and its consequences. These scientific revolutions are transformations of human consciousness, of the world view of an earlier age compared with that of modern thinking.

Thomas Kuhn[1] has shown that the determining reason for such radical changes is increasing tension between theory and fact, the appearance of anomalies, contradictions and irrationalities, beyond the scope of existing theories to explain. For the scientist these do not indicate that reality is too irrational for reason, but that *our* rational theories are inadequate to deal with the actual rationality of the universe. It becomes necessary when such situations develop to change the 'model', the theory. This is what was effected by Galileo with his new laws of motion and acceleration, and later by Newton; again by Darwin's theory of 'the Origin of the Species' and by Pasteur's germ theory of disease. Butterfield describes such fundamental revolutions in our thinking as 'picking up the other end of the stick'; Kuhn[2] called them 'changes in the paradigm', a paradigm shift—a paradigm being a model or pattern of thinking in terms of which all our concepts are formed just as all the forms of the verb in grammar are moulded on the standard paradigm of which they are examples or modifications.

As Kuhn sees it, the science of a particular period, operating with the accepted basic paradigm, works with a whole system of concepts together with its own logic. This constitutes the world as we see it at that time, and is not just a theory *about* that world. Of course that is exactly how Weber looks at his 'ideal type'. It is not a theory that we can *compare* with the world, for *we only know the world as seen through the grid of the model*; just as the medieval man saw the earth with its revolving spheres, not as a theory, but as reality itself. Kuhn points out that with the paradigm shift in science one world disappears and another takes its place.

There are, however, fundamental differences between the 'paradigm' in science and the 'model' for society.

(a) In science we have techniques for verification, and this gets us beyond the mere plausibility of a theory as making sense of the world for us, or giving us a good working scientific hypothesis to go on with.

(b) Again, in natural science the world we are examining does not appreciably change. The chemical and physical laws we use have been in operation, we have reason to believe, for the whole 4,000 million years of the earth's existence. But in society it is reality itself that is changing and not merely our theories about it.

(c) Man, the observer and theoriser, is also engaged in altering his world even as he observes it by his technology and his industrial and agricultural activities; and is constantly changing his forms of social organisation, his institutions and ideas, in order to adjust them to the requirements of these material changes.

We thus have two parallel but widely different forms of ideological change: the paradigm shift in natural science, and equally drastic reformations of society and its conceptual forms involving revolutionary changes in social relations, such as that from slavery to feudalism, in the economy, in political institutions, in the whole mental world which gives us what we take to be reality, and in the pattern of human conduct, moral codes and social patterns of living. These can be as different as the Indian caste system, feudal society, and modern capitalism.

In natural science we present ourselves with a new world, that of evolution, of genetics, of the micro-organism and disease, of quantum theory and relativity. As far as society is concerned many people, and especially the ideologists of the contemporary world, tend to believe that society is something 'given' once for all, much the same through the centuries in spite of change in dress, scientific views and customs. They are unwilling to face the fact that the transition from capitalism to socialism (a process, it should be noted, that no one supposes to be sudden—it might well continue for a century or more) carries with it as radical a transformation of human nature, of our social structure, our ethical standards, our values, our customs, and our conception of life as did the change in understanding nature when magic was superseded by modern science.

That being so, the sociologist, too, must never speak as though the theoretical world that reflects social data as we see them today was something permanent, as though there could only be the one objective social world we now know, and as though its laws and structure remain basically the same through all generations—so that we can have *a science of society as such*, as though social facts could be seen through, as it were, like transparent glass to perceive the structure of a world in principle always the same.

This sociological obsession with the *immediacy* of reality, as though reality had to be and could not be anything other than what we see before us at the moment, while it has some similarity with scientific conservatism, is much more stubborn and has even more unfortunate consequences. It arises from the fact that the successive social systems that have arisen in history have each been based on the creative work and ultimately, on the domination of a particular group or class whose interests, therefore, are closely bound up with its continued existence. It has frequently been the case that as one form becomes obsolete another develops to replace it, as industrialism replaced the earlier forms of feudal and mercantile society. In that case the threatened class defends its own form of society because it feels that its institutions are the basis of social reality.

The ideals and ideas, the principles and moral codes, the institutions and economic and political theories which have grown up with that society and have given it stability and significance are now its most powerful defence. Clearly such an ideology—the thought and feeling, the innermost spirit, of a whole civilisation—has a greater strength and stability than any scientific theory. Thus when a new social order appears, the paradigm shift becomes a lengthy and hard fought war of ideologies. The new order cannot establish itself merely as a new way of action *within* existing society. It is an assault on the whole structure of society, and needs to overthrow all its ideas and institutions in order to build its own, which are fundamentally different. This explains the bitter struggles involved when a paradigm shift takes place in the history of society.

It is difficult for the theorists of a declining society to realise that their own world is due for replacement and that the systems of law, of political theory, of the structure of society, of economics, of ethics and of philosophy are 'suffering a sea change into something rich and strange.' It seems to them that an attempt is being made to subvert nature itself. They have to learn that no historical form of consciousness can last longer than the passing and transitory phase of history that it represents. Its abstractions and concepts cannot usurp reality in its constant development. No culture, no civilisation, no economic system with its political and civic institutions, can claim such permanence. To assume as much is to hypostatise the evanescent, to create an ontology out of the transitory—a metaphysic of the nature of being.

It is seldom recognised that Weber made no such mistake. Rejecting any such naïve realism, he believed that all the forms of society are constituted by our own creative activity, and are derived from a basic model which is itself a construction of the mind, deriving its structure and principles from the point of view from which we create it. Thus all its law systems, principles, behaviour patterns and institutions are historically conditioned. According to Weber, they most certainly do not claim to represent reality. They are no more than reality *for us*.

History is a moving pageant; yet we take a single episode and insist that it is the truth for all time, its consciousness the pattern of human consciousness as such, as we might take a single negative or still from a film of rapid action, an instantaneous snapshot of the undivided mobility of the real. We try to catch, as in a net, the moving history as it passes, instead of grasping the historical sequence as the reality, and understanding the moment only in relation to that sequence, as explained by its past, and above all by what it is *becoming*, rather than by the *abstraction* of what it is now, what it momentarily, *is*.

The sociologist, observing the empirical facts, imagines himself to be standing on a fixed platform from which to await and observe the movement as it passes, instead of being where he is, *in* the moving process. He then reconstructs reality, which is all tendency and mobility, with percepts and concepts whose function it is to make it stationary. And all the while, posing as 'the pure visitor' standing outside reality, he is in fact one of the participants in its continuous modification.

This has happened before in history. It was manifest in the years of the decline of the Roman Empire, when it gave rise to a whole series of philosophies of withdrawal and despair—Stoicism, Epicureanism, and the retreat to monasticism. It occurred again in the break-up of the medieval synthesis; and once again when the Enlightenment attacked the supernatural sanctions and the irrational institutions of political absolutism.

We are in such a period of transition today. It is a time of bewilderment for many, of new beginnings for some. It is marked by an effort to make a last-ditch defence of the indefensible. But it is also a time for tearing down the veils which obscure and distort reality, the dispersal of the illusions of an epoch. Above all, it is an expansion of consciousness beyond the potential of bourgeois thought.

This process of disillusionment and ideological disintegration was well described by Plekhanov:

Every social institution is in the first case a form of development of productive forces. This, so to speak, is the best time of its life. It grows strong, develops and reaches its height. Instinctively people are attached to it and proclaim it 'sacred' or 'natural'. But gradually old-age comes on, decline sets in. They begin to notice that not everything about this institution is as splendid as once they thought. They begin to struggle against it, declare it 'against nature' and finally destroy it. This takes place because the productive forces of society are no longer what they once were; it takes place because they have already made a fresh step forward, thanks to which changes are taking place in the mutual relations of people and the social process of production.[3]

This paradigm shift involves the overthrow of the belief that capitalist forms of life, together with the imposing edifice of economic theory which is their basis, are immutable forms of nature. These cannot, however, be abolished by themselves but only along with the abolition by destructive criticism of the bourgeois consciousness which is their ideology. Both tasks must be linked with that of fighting for the satisfaction of the needs which are being denied by the working of the existing economy as incompatible with its laws and therefore impossible. Vital requirements in the way of houses, jobs, better schools, and many other things, well within the capacity of society to supply, are being withheld unnecessarily. This must not be tolerated; but along with the struggle, the ideological defence of this deprivation must be attacked, for victory is impossible so long as this ideology remains supreme.

The coincidence of consciousness and reality is the essence of dialectics. Ideas are not just a mirror image of material fact, economics and the actual system are parts of a world now in dissolution along with all its ideological forms (its legal, philosophical, cultural aspects) and its economic theory. Theoretical criticism and practical change are inseparable. All must be criticised and changed; criticised in theory and overthrown in action, together with the legal and political structure of society. A new consciousness the guiding principle and face of a single theoretical-practical and critical-revolutionary activity.[4]

It is a mistake to see this as mere 'superstructure' which will disappear once industrial and political power passes into new hands. Just as in economics, theory is inseparable from the operation of the business system, and inflation is a fact as well as a theory, so in every sphere form and content are inseparable. There must be as vigorous an onslaught on the consciousness, the ideas, assumptions, values and illusions of the existing system as upon its material basis. One cannot be expected to defeat the political power of capitalism imbued with its own values, illusions, and beliefs about human nature without defeating the ideology, the *consciousness* of the very class that is to be superseded.

As crisis deepens and criticism intensifies we must expect vigorous attempts to strengthen the bourgeois hold on the minds of men. Theories are given a new rigidity. The veil of obscurity thickens. There is not the least possibility of bourgeois comprehension of the real situation. The very survival of the class rests on the assumption that it never obtains a clear concept of the social preconditions of its own existence, or comes to regard its ideology as problematic.

The bourgeois consciousness is, in an abstract and formal view, at the same time also a distinct *unconsciousness.* . . . The falseness which is contained in this state of things is therefore nothing accidental, but precisely the expression of the mental plane of the objective structure. The limitations which make the class consciousness of the bourgeoisie a 'false' consciousness, is objective; it is the situation of the class itself. It is an objective consequence of the economic structure of society.[5]

The first prerequisite of advance beyond the limits of an outmoded order is therefore the realisation that the explanatory and justifying ideology, the reification of a passing historical form, is not part of the unalterable structure of the universe; it has no similarity to the conceptual systems of science. It is a form of consciousness with no more substantiality than the discarded forms of consciousness of the ages of superstition, and the Divine Right of Kings, of the spirits and controlling forces which filled nature for primitive man.

Bourgeois consciousness itself will never reach the point of questioning its own assumptions, of wanting to do things differently. It will look for solutions that attempt only to deal with the symptoms, and will put into effect remedies which affect matters at one point but create further and often worse difficulties elsewhere. This is the characteristic opportunism of a shallow reformism. On the other hand there may also be efforts to deal with the problem by seeking help from outside; by a moral appeal for more sympathy, for 'moral rearmament', for a spiritual revival; or, again, utopian proposals will be advanced, contrasting more satisfactory forms of society, 'alternative' societies, with present circumstances, and in some cases setting up small communities to lead the way. The more practical will believe that what is wanted is more effort, greater determination, vigorous political pressure, larger demonstrations, to overcome the hard-heartedness, the selfish complacency, the bureaucratic stubbornness which stands in the way of measures which could now, at once, be put into effect and would overcome the problem.

All such attempts that stop short of a deeper criticism and of measures that go beyond the limits set by the existing system can only end in disappointment. Nor will an increase in militancy by itself, least of all shouts for 'revolution now', show the real way forward.

Bourgeois forms of consciousness are not mere illusions but, in Marx's words, 'highly objective and highly practical social realities', and in consequence they must be criticised in theory and overthrown in practice together with the economic, legal, and political structures of society and at the same time.[6] This involves the fight for a new consciousness which is the understanding of a society now in the making, the guiding principle and force "of a single theoretical-practical and critical-revolutionary action".[7]

The world does not change automatically, ideas and ideologies merely following material change as a reflection of already achieved reality. There is no change at all until men understand its necessity and consciously direct the reconstruction of society. Truth is not arrived at *post facto*, a reflection of what is; it is the effective reshaping of the facts; it initiates change in existing reality, it does not copy it.

Such an advance can never be at its beginning that of a whole class which has awakened to a true understanding of its situation and has emancipated itself from the paralysing illusions of bourgeois society. It can only follow the appearance, as a first step, of a creative minority. But if the higher level of consciousness of this minority represents the *potential* consciousness of the majority, the struggle in which the advance group takes the lead, carried on simultaneously on the practical and the theoretical field, will carry forward the whole class, stage by stage, until the majority have risen to the same level as the minority.

Such a step forward can only take place when all the conditions demand it. People are never moved to break the crust of custom, to stir out of their ordinary way of living, out of the lethargy of things-as-they-are, unless they are confronted by a situation which they must meet and overcome at the peril of complete disaster, and which therefore rouses them to make an unprecedented effort.

Once such a movement begins, it acquires a momentum that carries it a step further; from achievement to a fresh struggle, from the solution of one problem to the presentation of another, from stagnation and despair to reiterated movement.

Such a situation appears at a time when imminent impoverishment threatens at the same time as economic potential increases. In confronting this crisis we are seriously limited by the 'objective possibilities' of the system as represented by economic law; this constitutes our present consciousness and its potential. Weber is well aware that this range of possibilities belongs not to economic reality as such, as would be the case in the fields covered by the natural sciences, but to the economic laws of his 'ideal type', which is a mental construct from one chosen point of view, that of the existing bourgeoisie. Quite a different model could be framed on the basis of a *developed* economy and from the point of view of the community and its needs. Such a model would have a much wider range of objective possibilities which would allow us to transcend the limits of the existing system. In such circumstances we are compelled to regard the whole system of consciousness which restricts our efforts as a 'false consciousness'. It was, of course, not that in the days when it was a progressive form of thought and action, playing its historical role in developing production to new heights. It is only when, having done so, the same system proves inappropriate to the full use of the powers it has developed, that it becomes not only obsolete but a grave peril to society, and its ideology becomes a 'false consciousness'.

It is sometimes argued that every form of consciousness is an ideology and a 'false consciousness'; that the alternative conceptual model is only that of another class, seeing things from an alternative point of view and with its own sectional values. In the past, radical social change has indeed represented only the appearance of another class and it has advanced only an ideology that represented the interests of that class. Even so, it also represented a genuine advance and in many ways widened the sphere of liberty and developed the means of life for all. In every case, limited aims were advanced under the appeal for ideals of complete generality, such as 'liberty, equality and fraternity'. This, however, is an indication that the whole process is inspired by universal human betterment, and that it is not impossible that the time may arrive when the first real steps to the emancipation of all mankind become a genuine possibility.

This would appear to be the case when, instead of a sectional interest, such as that frankly confessed by capitalism (general welfare being a by-product), what is proposed is the rational disposal and utilisation of resources as the direct aim of the economy, while at the same time no economic structure is proposed which, like that of Weber, begins by asserting the necessity for the class ownership of the means of production and a political system of domination to maintain a confessed system of class ownership and privilege. What is now on the agenda of history as the only way to secure direct rational control of resources is not another class rule, but the end of economic classes by means of the general ownership and utilisation of resources.

At no previous stage of history has it been possible or even been claimed that the whole historical process is envisaged, so as to put the past and the present in their place and proceed to create the future. It is only as a result of successful capitalist development that mankind gains for the first time an understanding of the sequence of technological and organisational advances which makes history visible. Previous epochs were definitely limited in their perspective, as Weber frankly acknowledges his own to be. This must not be regarded as blameworthy. Such class systems served an historical purpose and carried society on to a higher stage. But none of them saw their activities as a link in the progressive mastery of the earth's resources and a developing rationalisation of the economic process not for sectional but for general welfare. It is only now that we have arrived at a position from which the whole development of society becomes clear. It is capitalism that by its own universality, its overcoming of so many obstacles, social, political, ideological and institutional, has already socialised production and made society the reality for man. But the class that has achieved this has so involved its own interests in the present structure that it has incapacitated itself for carrying out its own development and fulfilment. This blinds it to the existing situation, to an understanding of present reality. Only those who are willing to usher in the future can see the concrete truth of the present.

The *actual* consciousness of the working class is not fundamentally different from that of the bourgeoisie who, as Marx says, "as thinkers and as producers of ideas, regulate the production and distribution of the ideas of their age". They control the media, education, broadcasting and publishing. The 'ideal types', their values, are generally accepted and imitated. Yet in several ways the present consciousness of the workers begins to differentiate itself definitely from the general unanimity. In the first place, economic and social changes are already in process which point beyond the accepted picture of things. There are changes in capitalism itself: the increased participation of government in finance and control; expectations of the workers as to incomes and security and holidays abroad, as to facilities for sport and recreation, and as to ability to buy domestic appliances and clothes and furnish their houses adequately, all of which go far beyond the expectations of only a few decades ago. Secondly there are evidences of new thinking, of criticism and disillusionment, especially with politicians and the establishment and the ruling personnel. There is not nearly the same willingness to accept their word on what is possible, right and proper, or on what has to be accepted as inevitable. What is happening is that the new is not only in the future, something which does not exist and is excluded by the dominance of the bourgeois authority, but is already here and growing up amid the decline and disintegration of the old. "In reality", said Lenin, "socialism looks out at us now through all the windows of present-day capitalism; the outline of socialism appears before us *in practice*."[8] Though some of these elements are relatively minor as yet, they have within them the promise of the future.

Thus while the bourgeoisie and the workers see the same capitalist society, and to a large extent have come to terms with it, the bourgeoisie are imprisoned within it, while the workers are forced to go beyond it, and are discovering that they have only to liberate elements of the new society that have already grown up within the capitalist world.

While the bourgeoisie remain enmeshed in the web of the existent, which it takes to be all that is or can be, the working class must in the end be driven to abandon it or go down into the "general ruin of the contending forces" which Marx held to be the only alternative to socialism.

NOTES

1. T. Kuhn, *Revolutions in Science*.
2. Ibid.
3. Karl Korsch, *Marxism and Philosophy*.
4. Ibid.
5. G. Lukacs, *History and Class Consciousness*.
6. See V. I. Lenin, *On the Significance of Militant Materialism*.
7. Karl Korsch, *Marxism and Philosophy*.
8. V. I. Lenin, *The Threatening Catastrophe*. See also K. Marx, *Capital*, vol. 3, ch. 27.

14

The Making of History

The strength of Max Weber's position, seldom appreciated by those who do no more than make use of portions of his methodology—he is rich in suggestive contributions both for research and theoretical work in sociology—is that he grasps the basic values as well as the economic concepts of the capitalist epoch. This the empiricists never did. Strong in their refusal to indulge in speculative theories, in their determination to be scientific and realistic, they failed in their comprehension of capitalism as a *Weltanschauung*, as a world view, a phase of civilisation as a whole—its industry, its social structures, its philosophy, its institutions, its ethics and its culture. In this Weber is Kantian, as well as in the use of his 'model' to grasp the theoretical structure of society. Kant found the comprehension of social reality not through his categorial system, which dealt with scientific reality, but through the grasp of moral reality by intuition. For Weber this was to be advanced by understanding 'the spirit of capitalism', an essentially value-oriented social reality. Capitalism thus appears historically, as a new form of society with its own value categories and its corresponding structural organisation.

The naïve empiricism of the sociologists, who have not

yet discovered their own presuppositions, and have not recognised the fact that their thinking is in the categories of the capitalist epoch, fails to realise the historical relativity of their thinking. Weber's superiority to them is that he fully recognises that the capitalist system—its civilisation, its policies, its ethics and its culture (again we insist on this)—is *not reality in itself* but *reality-for-us*, our subjective and even arbitrary world view. We *choose* our basic value attitudes, he says, and the whole structure of our thinking, feeling and behaviour follows and depends on that choice. Weber bases everything on the mental pattern or 'ideal type' which is the consciousness of our time, and which defines the necessities and the possibilities of our actual world.

But Weber does not realise that he has constructed a model which is only valid for the current historical situation; and that the time must come, as for us it has come, to go beyond its limits, and to escape its bondage.

We do not, however, effect this change either by appealing for a better way of ordering our economic life, or by 'piecemeal social engineering', on the one hand, or by 'smashing the system', or letting it smash itself, and then starting from scratch to build a socialist society, on the other.

The way forward is indicated in the new features, the straining possibilities, the tendencies we discern, in highly developed capitalism itself. If we take the historical perspective we see the capitalist era as an objective phenomenon, arising by human ingenuity, intelligence, and creative originality over a period of some 200 years, first to create a new industrial mechanism based on the machine and at the same time to reorganise the capital-labour relationship on the basis of the wage system; then to bring law and government into line, and finally to radicalise the moral and cultural thinking of society.

This makes the Kantian model—both on its rational and value sides—an *historical* phenomenon. We see its 'reason', not in terms of abstract categories of scientific thought, but in terms of man's building of his world and the successive stages in the mastery of nature through science, technology and industry. Each period has seen the creation of a new world of technology, of industrial and agricultural production, and at the same time a society with new values, new institutions and a new culture. As Weber comprehends it, this is an extension of the principle of rationalisation, so clearly seen in the mathematical exactness of modern science and technology, and the strict accounting of modern business. But the basic differentia are in the capitalist forms of social relationship—the wage system, the investment system, the money game and its culture, as represented, for instance, in the business supplements of the daily papers on the side of its infrastructure and in the coloured supplements of the Sunday papers on the side of its superstructure.

No historical period endures for ever. A new era appears only when one stage creates not only the problems of its hypertrophy, but creates at the same time a possibility of emerging beyond its contradictions, and, moreover, the necessity of doing so. Marx said that the problem of radical change does not appear on the agenda of history until "the material conditions necessary for its solution already exist or are, at least, in the process of formation". Until then our world view is limited by the concepts of the existing order.

Consciousness remains ideologically bound as long as it is powerless. It is no longer in bondage when the conditions are such that there is both a grave social crisis, and at the same time a way forward. Only *then* can thought envisage a paradigm shift.

The conception of an *ideology* is that it is the limited consciousness bound to *what is* and therefore limited to existing categories, excluding, therefore, the possibility of conceiving the transformation of the basic structure of society. Bound to the earlier stage, it is not realised that the movement which created it has in fact produced the embryo of another movement, radically different, and going beyond it.

There is nothing in this conception, of an evolutionary force relentlessly unfolding the historical sequence. The fact that candles came before gaslight, and gaslight before electric light, is not a highly questionable metaphysic, it is an empirical line of progress. Nor is there a one-line deterministic sequence of technology and social forms. Nor is technology the basis of social advance, a form of technological determinism; for it is ideas and the influence of culture, even of religion (as Weber shows) and philosophy, that develops the technology. Once again we have to get away from false dichotomies of ideas and social institutions, as if these were on separate levels. There is *one* reality, and that is *man working on his material environment*. When he thinks, he thinks to act. When he acts, it makes him think again on the basis of the new situation he has created.

This was the discovery of Giovanni Vico, to whom Marx was indebted for many of his views: that man only knows what he makes and what he has modified. He knows the world that he himself has created. This explains how it is that consciousness is what relates to the on-going historical process; is a component of the successive social forms of history, and is at the same time creatively operative. Reality, as we know it, as it appears in our civilisation, is man-made, man-controlled, goal-directed. It is above all the creation of intelligent thinking.

This is most manifest, and most indispensable, in those times when man changes the course of history—not because such a change is determined, not because it happens automatically, but because it can only happen on the basis of an intelligent grasp of a critical situation, of *new thinking*. There has been no adequate recognition of the part which human beings have played in history in reacting upon, altering and transforming their environment. Neither 'materialism', nor the view that man is conditioned by social and environmental pressures, nor the obsession with the directly observed fact *abstracted from the time process*, could account for the redirective activity of man, for the actualities of human thinking and its creative results. Empiricism gets no farther than reflective perception of what has already happened and that is a form of knowledge, however elaborate, detailed, generalised, that is impotent to affect the course of things, to bring about radical social change.

Redirective activity demands the appearance of a higher *potential consciousness* impossible to those enveloped in and subjugated by the ideology of the present age. It arises when society comes up against a barrier it cannot surmount as long as it follows existing modes of thought, and surmounts only when it grasps that the development of its own system points beyond the limits of contemporary consciousness and, in our day, bourgeois consciousness.

The theoretical edifice of economics, political theory and sociology is extensive, complex, carefully constructed and impressive. It is the achievement of rational thinking, an integrated whole in which the economic basis subtends the complex social structure, so well described by Talcott Parsons and later developed by contemporary political and social theory.

But social reality has failed to live up to social theory. Everywhere it reveals irrationalities, discord, anarchy and economic confusion, areas of unredeemed alienation, poverty and discontent. As Kierkegaard says, ''We have constructed a magnificent palace, but the hovels of the real world exist despite the speculative edifice built by the theorists.'' Of course our civilisation has its oases of graceful living and polished culture, its pleasant communities and hosts of decent people, but the structure is unsound—a *Titanic* with its first and second class passengers in the saloons, but holed below the water-line, and the third class passengers drowning in the steerage.

This is a contradiction that provokes the emergence of a

critical consciousness to confront the complacency of structural functionalism. It appears in the years when a once-powerful system is reaching its end and is turning downwards in decline. Such periods of crisis have occurred before in the history of Western Europe. Man is not wholly conditioned by circumstances. He can react *against* them to create new circumstances beyond the frustrations and decadence of his time, and in doing so changes his own nature too.[1] Thought, if it is really thought, creates new forms of being, transcending existing conditions and their thinking.

We see in this criticism and reframing of the concepts whereby we comprehend the world the process whereby society becomes more rational, a truer consciousness overcoming the false consciousness of a less rational form of society.

When we know how to control nature for our needs by economic means subject to rational control as well as technologically, history ceases to be determined by the kind of laws resulting from the mere interaction of innumerable personal and gain-seeking wills under the capitalist model, and is controlled by ourselves.

Man at earlier stages did not know that he had to continue this form of world development, and did not understand the total process as we can now. In our day the rationality of history is perceived. It is seen as within the historical process not as an evolutionary force, but as a process requiring *our* criticism, and our redirection of the course of things.

Man and his world, subject and object, are seen as united and not a dichotomy (with all its insuperable difficulties). The gradual mastery of nature and rationalising of society is part of the critical and practical unification of the world, of completing internally, within the unity, the rational aim of society.

The future of the world, then, depends on *a true consciousness*—by which one means seeing this process and our part in it, as now in our generation, for the first time in history, we are able to do. The logic of history therefore becomes a *practical* question, not a metaphysical question as to how rational the world really is in spite of its apparent irrationality. In history men have not known the consequences for the future of what they were doing, they were ideologically circumscribed. We pass beyond ideology because we do know the consequences, because we envisage them as our plan and aim, and therefore deliberately make our own history.

We do not therefore observe the workings of a system of which we are only the observers. Our sociology and our philosophy of history is not a doctrine, not a philosophy, but a participation in the on-going business of our world.

Each historical phase has in the past been a form of domination, from slavery to that so clearly defined by Weber and Parsons. There have been in the past protests and revolts on many occasions, always ineffectual but at times leading to another, though more progressive, form of domination; but now we can envisage complete emancipation as a real possibility, because the potentiality of modern industry no longer requires, as it did in every previous age, the forced deprivation of the majority and the good life only for the ruling classes.

The now visible goal is of the fullest development of economic potentialities and human individuality. The alternative, if we remain within the limits of contemporary consciousness and the established forms of society, if we submit to the sociology of things as they are, can be nothing but *adjustment* to the tyranny of capitalist concepts and the interests they represent. If we go beyond these forms we go beyond the socially defined potentialities to new modes of personality and individuality, beyond the *adjusted type* necessitated by existing limits.

It is not enough to direct criticism against these immediate pressures, to rebel against restraints and adjustments while accepting the pressure of the criticised society—which is the error of all reformism, whether Labour or professing to be Marxist. To oppose the structure is to oppose those whose structure it is. Who made it to do what it is doing to serve their interests? It is to oppose, and to overthrow their domination.

The enlightened individual is the prisoner of outside forces; but he now knows that they are *his* forces, since man himself made the society which is now his enemy, and man himself can once again, in the long story of civilisation, remake his world.

It becomes clear that there are two sociologies. The first proclaims its aim as to see things as they are and subject to their own laws. In this case, as the critics of structural functionalism have pointed out, sociology envisages no possibility of change—for it rules that out by the very definition of a structure designed to maintain its order, its equilibrium and its wholeness by subordinating every part to the demands of the whole—the pattern of Talcot Parsons' society, and most sociological systems since his *Structure of Social Action*. This gives us a total relativity of as many distinct societies as history provides us with, each a self-contained whole. There is no rational theory of history here and no meaning in history.

If, however, we see the rational power of man operating through the sequence of phases involved in man's control of nature and of economic forces, we can see the sequence of societies as reflecting definite levels of production and, therefore, as rational, as making sense. On this basis we can develop a rational sociology and a philosophy of history, not as a speculative theory, not as an explanation from without, but as a growing consciousness *within* history of what it is all about. This is not seeing the whole from outside, but from inside.

This is not to abandon theory. But theory becomes the operating plan of "work in progress during alterations". We grasp the world theoretically in order to change it. It means:

Knowing that we are in a period of historical crisis:
Knowing that capitalism represents *one* passing phase in history;
Knowing that social history, economic and cultural, is the growing control by, man, passing into full and *conscious* control of the economy and the alternative is disaster.

To reach this understanding is to pass beyond ideologies, not to absolute truth, which is simply an absurd phrase, but to the comprehension of the significance, not just of our present world as such, but of our world in its sequence of forms and of the possibility of seeing it as it has never before been seen in history, and playing our constructive part in the redirection of events. It is *this* understanding that goes beyond ideology.

The logic of history is man's power to produce his own world. In the course of this history man masters nature and brings it under his control, modifies nature and puts himself, his intelligence, his values, into the visible world of machines, buildings, cathedrals, pictures, parks, music, theories and poems and philosophies that he creates to confront him as *humanised* externality. He transcends himself as natural man transcends nature in himself. By shaping it to his own requirements he modifies himself in his own activity and creates fresh needs and goals and ambitions for himself. He progresses by resolving in action the problems created by his own previous activity. And this is nothing more and nothing less than what Marx means by dialectics.

The logic is the actual process itself. It is the intervention of consciousness, as understanding: first, as consciousness of negation, of obstruction, of frustration; second, as criticism—of the economic system, of the superstructure, of the class monopoly and rule in its own interests, of impending disaster; third, as the necessity of going beyond the limits of existing ideas, theories, inevitabilities and possibilities, because all the conditions and concrete realities have prepared it and demand it.

Such action takes us beyond the law system of the bourgeois world, beyond the rules of the game, beyond its language and conceptual forms, above all beyond 'the illusions of the epoch' which all these 'forms of thought' constitute, its veil, its opaqueness, its absurdity, its irrationality. It is essentially a positive move in the direction of freedom.

But has man power to do so conditioned and moulded by the ideological pressures of a bourgeois world, creating education and culture wholly after the pattern of its own acquisitive aims, money values, and domination? Marx pointed out that there is not just 'human nature', something fixed, through all time; on the contrary:

The whole of history is nothing but a continual transformation of human nature. By acting on the world and changing it, he at the same time changes his own nature and develops the potentialities that slumber within him. In acquiring new productive forces men change their mode of production, and in changing their mode of production, their manner of gaining a living they change all their social relations. The windmill gives us society with the feudal lord; the steam mill society with the industrial capitalist. The same men who establish social relations conformably with their material productivity, produce also the principles, the ideas, the categories, conformably with their social relations. . . . These are historical and transitory products . . . there is nothing immutable but the abstraction of the movement.[2]

A sociology which by its own epistemology can be no more than a rejection of existing structure can only go on demanding more and more insistently conformism and submission on the part of dissident elements. The really serious problem for contemporary sociology is the problem of deviance. Talcott Parsons had hoped to contain it by the ideological pressure of the structural procedures which he called 'internalisation'; König aptly describes it as the "auto-domestication of humanity". This, it is claimed, will give "the optimal development of a person's potentiality and the realisation of his individuality".

This is precisely what, under the pressure of conformity to the sickness of an acquisitive society, is essentially unattainable, because the inner conflict of established civilisation itself in its very structure denies it, as Weber, Tönnies and Simmel firmly insist.

Either one finds 'personality' and 'individuality' in terms of their possibilities *within* the established form of civilisation, in which case their realisation is for the vast majority tantamount to successful adjustment. Or one defines them in terms of their transcending content, including their socially denied potentialities beyond their actual existence; in this case their realisation would imply transgression beyond the established form of civilisation, to radically new modes of 'personality' and 'individuality' incompatible with the prevailing ones. Today this would mean curing the patient to become a rebel.[3]

Of course, it is to prevent this that deviance has to be vigorously combated, internalisation stepped up, and, according to Talcott Parsons, coercion resorted to where this fails. Meanwhile the pressure of rational theory, of value-free science, is increased. Precisely because man has never come so close to the fulfilment of his hopes, he has never been so strictly restrained from fulfilling them.

This places the whole responsibility on man to escape from the dilemma in which he has involved himself. He has done so a hundred times in history. But not *all* men on *every* occasion have taken the way forward, but *some* have. While the rest fell back into stagnation or succumbed;

overwhelmed by military or economic disaster, some did have the courage and the intelligence to go forward. Today some men seek escape by 'retreat into the interior' of the personality, by hopes for the realisation of man's possibilities in another life, or in the indefinite future. While he waits to be saved he obeys the dictators of the dominating social power, the victim of a society in manifest decay. For the fulfilment of his destiny a new consciousness is needed, tenacious, rational and sceptical, in order to unmask the fetishes, the hobgoblins, the ruthless law-enforcement of the economy, the legal enforcement of the social order. To put an end to this situation and bring society in line with the already created forces thrusting towards realisation, man has got to transcend the social structure which subordinates one class to another and overcome the economic organisation in which the worker is only an instrument of production. To do this men, the groups and strata, the individuals and unions, which know that they must go forward, have to become conscious both of the political and ideological transformation in which, willy nilly, they are actually involved. History will not wait for a leisurely theoretical education. Man is educated by being called to the first, limited, intelligent step *in a new direction, against* all that he is told that he *must* do. This action is enormously educative. Marx always pointed out that man is not to be re-educated completely *before* the struggle, but is re-made, has his illusions knocked out of him one by one, discovers new ideas, new possibilities, new powers in himself, *in the course of the struggle* and in no other way.

For the working class it is a matter of life and death that they become aware of the real situation, and of the practicability and the necessity of carrying the socio-historical process on to the next stage. To the bourgeoisie the rational control of production for use is so completely beyond the stage of their potential consciousness as to be wholly utopian and absurd. The future depends on men who can penetrate the obvious which is false, and formulate the paradox which is true. This authentic thinking is that which breaks through the limits of capitalism to grasp the historical process that puts the past and the present in their place and proceeds to create the future.

This is possible because those not wholly involved in the capitalist process at the owning-class end, find their existence endangered by its continuance, and develop a political consciousness that can go beyond Weber's 'objective possibilities' as seen by the limited potentials of capitalist ideology and by those so situated in society as to be dominated by it under all circumstances. The question is whether any group or class can extend its consciousness beyond that. This would be possible only when such a group or class finds that its interests can only be achieved, and its safety and welfare secured, by going beyond the economic possibilities of capitalism.

NOTES

1. K. Marx, *Theses on Feuerbach*, No. 3.
2. From K. Marx *Capital*, vol. 1, ch. 5, and *The Poverty of Philosophy*.
3. H. Marcuse, *Eros and Civilisation*

15

Sociology and the Politics of Cultural Despair

The profound pessimism of Weber and his colleagues Tönnies and Simmel is revealing. Coming as they did at the summit of the authority of capitalism, they were not of those who looked at the present with complacency or the future with hope as they contemplated 'the ideal type'—its structure, and its functional apparatus of economic laws and bureaucratic domination.

The years before the first world war looked eagerly forward. It was the time of the confident philosophy of men like Bernard Bosanquet, the British 'Hegelian', who argued that the rational 'absolute', was more 'real' than the world as it appears. The eternal order of truth and righteousness *which now is* gives a moral and legal justification to our ordered society and its necessary class differentiation. The ultimate truth of what *appears* evil is that it plays its part in the service of the good.

Weber took a hard, contemptuous look at stuff like that: "The ultimate and most sublime values", he declares, "have retreated from public life into the transcendental realms of mystic life."[1] His vision of the future was very different and bears a disconcerting resemblance to Spengler's *Decline of the West*, published in 1918, which declared war "the eternal form of the highest human existence", denied historical progress and saw the nineteenth century as the modern world entering its period of decline. Weber could see no alternative to the systematic fostering of an élite on whom the dreadful responsibility of government would devolve. From their ranks there would arise a charismatic party leader who would govern with dictatorial powers. He did not know that this individual was already on the scene as a corporal in the Austrian Army—his name was Adolf Hitler, and he was perfectly to embody Weber's principle of 'Führerdemokratie', plebiscite and all.

Pareto, the Italian sociologist who became a devoted supporter of Mussolini, saw the world as controlled by the irrational forces of instinct and passion, which *used* the logic and science of law and economics for their own irrational ends. This of necessity ruled out all considerations of an ethical nature or concern for human welfare which might stand in the way.

Pareto saw the basic political conflict as between two forces, both manifestations of instinctive power: these are *the foxes*, who win by cunning, and secondly, *the lions* who win the final victory by strength.

The whole modern élitist tradition with its culmination in authoritarian dictatorship derives from Weber and his successor Pareto.

The crushing defeat of Germany in the first world war and the threat of a Marxist sequel brought Weber in those years right into the political struggle. He was summoned to Vienna to address the Officer Corps on socialism in 1918.[2] In Munich his political speeches created a sensation. He seemed marked for that leading political role to which his commanding personality and powerful oratory seemed to fit him. He entered the field of political controversy and manoeuvre at the end of the war, to hold back the flood tide of revolution if he could. But he was at heart profoundly discouraged, the problematic character of rationality in the Western world tormented him. Where was it leading humanity? His intellectual struggle became intense. Bewildered and disappointed, he relinquished his participation after, as a final effort, giving his support to the defeat of the revolution by the Social Democratic leader Noske and the Army. World weariness overcame him, and he withdrew into his study. When in June, 1926, he was taken ill, he did not fight his illness and on June 14 he lay dead.[3]

The feeling of all deep thinkers in years following the first world war was not one of cheerful optimism but of profound disillusionment. They sensed a deep-seated disease at the heart of society. The spiritual decay was reflected in Ezra Pound's poetry:

> There died a myriad
> And of the best among them,
> For an old bitch gone in the teeth,
> For a botched civilisation,
> For two gross of broken statues,
> For a few thousand battered books,

and in the deep sense of irretrievable defeat in T. S. Eliot's *The Waste Land*:

> I could not speak.
> And my eyes failed, I was neither
> Living nor dead, and I know nothing.
> Looking into the heart of light, the silence.

Throughout Germany the destructive element dominated intellectual life in the widely read works of Ernst Jünger, Ludwig Klages, Paul Lagarde, Möller van der Bruck, Othman Spann, and many more.[4] Fritz Stern has shown in his study of the rise of the Germanic ideology how the deep pessimism of Weber and the irrationalism of Pareto and Spengler came to dominate the sociological consciousness of Germany and to spread beyond its frontiers throughout the whole Western world.[5]

In Britain, however, a complacent optimism still prevailed in the social sciences. Sociology made considerable headway in developing its empiricist methods. It remained, therefore, a purely descriptive science. That is to say, non-explanatory. Its special tasks were classification and the study of those internal changes in the given structure of society known as transformations, their constant features, relationships and uniformities. Its work had therefore become largely statistical and monographic, and precluded the comprehension of historical processes. The monographic method has been described as "much ado about very little", and as probably the best way to obscure the horizon of the real problems confronting society today. Its work is without exception unrelated in any way to the social and historical infra-structure.

Bourgeois thought in decline is incompatible with theories which are concerned with social change. Indeed, the very principle of the structural functionalism now generally accepted is that society maintains its order, and for every working unit its internalised expectation is geared to that end. Talcott Parsons consistently argues that the only type of empirical generalisation which can be validated is 'correlational' and 'probabilistic'. "General theory of the processes of change is not possible in the present state of knowledge."[6]

It could be said that the leading figures in contemporary sociology share a common ahumanistic, ahistorical and aphilosophical attitude. All of them appear to favour, explicitly or implicitly, the current technocratic society. S. M. Lipsett in *The Setting of Sociology in the 1950's* sees sociology today as

become emancipated from philosophy, less problem-oriented, less vital, less concerned, less committed, less historical, less humanistic, more sterile, and more conservative politically.

In method it appears to show excessive abstraction and over-preoccupation with methodology, while functionalism becomes an endorsement of the status quo and a body of study whose primary task is to deflect possible sources of criticism of society.

The preoccupation in sociology with social stability has developed a main concern with the ways through which society is maintained and its functional equilibrium guaranteed. A three-fold typology of deviant behaviour as pressing towards disequilibrium and change classifies the trouble-makers as motivated by (*a*) *retreatism*, (*b*) *rebellion*, (*c*) *innovation*. Dubin has found even more deviant types: in fact he describes twelve types of psychological abnormality which manifest potentialities for social change.

We have already referred to Professor König's definition of sociology as "the process of the social auto-domestication of humanity". Professor B. F. Skinner is ready with offers of help here. Pointing out that discussion, persuasion and argument are wasteful of time and ineffective, he suggests that what we should do is make use of 'contingency reinforcements', a method of conditioning which he has found effective with both pigeons and rats. To deal with the deviant

We need only to design contingencies under which the rebellions of youth can acquire behaviour that is useful to their society, contingencies that do not have a troublesome by-product.[7]

Consider the implications for deviance. If there is no reality other than the completed functional whole and we are concerned with its homeostasis, its equilibrium, any departure from this alloted role, any expectations and demands beyond the objectives possible for the system, must be regarded as abnormal, pathological. But to forbid conflict with the appointed role and with the rules necessary to preserve equilibrium may be tyrannical in a society which has failed to bring the general interest into line with justifiable individual interests; in which case rebellion may be less indicative of personal maladjustment than a genuine incompatability of private welfare and the requirements of the system, especially if Weber's analysis is accepted.

Consider the example given by Professor Hayek in his *Individualism True and False*. Effective functioning of the economy, in terms of the necessary profitability without which it ceases to operate, requires the submission of the workers to their role and the strict limitation of their expectations and demands. These must not interfere with the objective working of the rational mechanism.

Unfortunately, deviant individuals do not accept the necessity of submitting to the anonymous and seemingly irrational forces of society which must demand a readiness to adjust themselves to changes which may profoundly affect their fortunes and opportunities, the causes of which may be altogether unintelligible to them. This craving for intelligibility produces illusory demands which no system can satisfy and increasing unwillingness to bow before rules where utility is not rationally demonstrated.[8]

This is precisely Weber's "substantive irrationality": the operation of a value-free system which inflicts hardship and deprivation but which *must* be accepted, and not be resented on the irrelevant grounds of justice and humanity. Thus reason becomes unreason, and it is *unreason* we impose in its name.

Of course every society requires acceptance of obligations; but Rousseau was right when he insisted that obligations should be such as may be freely accepted because they manifestly secure and defend the welfare of each person in the community. But too often what is proclaimed as the common good is the imposition of a sectional interest to which the governed have to submit, always of course on the grounds that "what is good for General Motors is good for America", and that what is good for capitalism must be good for each and every worker.

But the deviants may be those who no longer accept the necessity for enforced deprivation, because in their view the system has reached a degree of development at which social reorganisation to secure better 'fortune and opportunity' not *worse*, to satisfy perfectly reasonable and intelligible demands, is both feasible and indeed necessary. Of course there are those who fall short of the reasonable restraints and obligations of every society; but the sociologists, and the public, must distinguish between those who fall below the level of social responsibility and those who feel that responsibility *more* than the sociologists, *more* than the general public, and are trying to bring society into line with the requirements of the economy itself. Persistence in maintaining the present system when all the developing forces of society are moving towards reorganisation means not the stability and equilibrium the sociologist demands, and believes that he can get by enforcing submission, but disequilibrium to the point of disintegration. It is only *readjustment* that secures equilibrium—and that can only be on a new level of social organisation.

But in every department of sociology we find the exclusion of the historical perspective, the refusal to see present facts as part of a changing reality, only to be understood in terms of its past and of the future it points to. If society has to be accepted as it is, all radical criticism and demands for radical change are resisted; but if society is seen as a process in which man is seeking all the time to improve his life through a higher technology and *repeated reorganisation* of the structure to attain higher, levels of rationality in a more equitable distribution of the produce of industry, then the sense of the need for change, the demand for reorganisation, will be seen as not pathological but as the healthy consciousness of society in process of change taking possession of people's minds.

But this is not appreciated when the historical dimension is excluded. No social phenomenon can be understood except in terms of its place in a developing society. From that point of view its significance takes on a totally different meaning from that in which its context in the process of becoming is ignored.

It is characteristic of all forms of empiricism that they fall short of attempting theoretical understanding. The 'hard fact' man scorns all theory as unnecessary and irrelevant—except, of course, for the naive theory that simple observation is the true account of reality. The functionalist goes as far as integrating the facts into an organic whole; but there he stops, and refuses to ask how the social whole came into being and for what reason.

The functionalist takes *any* existing system, at any time, for granted, though it may be a flagrant example of an organised system of privilege and exploitation or a very unstable system in its period of disintegration and change. Finally comes attributing the origin of the system to the working of western rational thought—but this goes no farther than the reply of the Indian philosopher to someone who inquired the origin of the world and who replied that it rested on the back of an elephant. When the inquirer, dissatisfied, asked: "And what about the elephant?", the philosopher replied: "Oh, the elephant rests on the back of a tortoise!" Whereupon the man went happily away. In the same style Weber never gets farther than the tortoise. His explanation of capitalism gets as far as 'Western rationalism', and the rational spirit of 'Protestantism': but is this really enough?

It is typical of a certain type of thinking to be satisfied with high-sounding abstractions which really explain nothing. To say that capitalism is 'rational' is perfectly true—we have the tortoise; but a real explanation will place capitalism in the series of socio-economic systems occasioned by man's increasing mastery of nature to satisfy his needs and allow them to enlarge. Here is the basis of a theory relating the pattern of social organisation to the level of the achieved technology. Thus we arrive at the economic changes which call for capitalism as the appropriate form of organisation at a certain level of industrial advance. It is along these lines that we arrive at a real theory of the origin and at the same time of the nature and structure of equilibrium.

For Weber, reason stops short at the single system —capitalism, as though the whole of history were not the march of intelligence in the control of nature and the organisation of forms of society corresponding to the successive stages of economic and technological progress.

Theory gets nowhere if it stops at mere description of what now is, at classification, and a few generalisations. Early botany did little more than observe, describe and classify plants. This was well worth doing; but scientific botany did not begin until the flowering plant was *understood* in its cell structure and vascular system, its metabolism, its photosynthesis, its tropisms, and above all in its *comparative* anatomy—setting it in its place in the developmental progress from the non-flowering fern type of plant and the mosses which preceded the fern. All biological understanding is based on comparative studies which are at the same time evolutionary studies. It is the succession that explains the modifications of the chordate basic structure of skeleton, circulation, nervous system and excretory system as these are developed and modified from the original basic structures. *This is theory*; and it is a lot more than description, or classification, or generalisation based on what we *now* observe.

There is no science without theory, and sociology is disastrously lacking in theory of the explanatory scientific kind; to such an extent that theory and research are often regarded as separate and independent activities. The farthest explanation gets is to arrive at the structural functionalism of a society; but it cannot tell us how it arose and refuses to allow that it can ever change. How far would that take us in biology?

If in all organic questions an evolutionary standpoint is necessary and, further, if in all human life the intelligence of men in devising techniques and then in social organisations to operate those techniques is basic to the development and functioning of social structure, it follows that sociology as a science of society must have an historical dimension; and that is what is lacking in contemporary sociology. We have not understood capitalist society, however carefully we have mapped its class-structure, until we have put it in the series of class-structured social forms corresponding to the development of technology over the past 5,000 years. That no more implies an evolution through any preordained series than the fact that the hydra or coelenterate form precedes the annelid, the annelid the chordate and the chordate the vertebrate means that each inevitably developed into the next in the sequence. Yet just that sequence is the explanation of animal development.

The theory that we find available is not a linear theory of imminent evolutionary teleology, driving society to a predetermined end; nor is it Dilthey's or Spengler's or Toynbee's theory of an endless cycle of arbitrary forms, or simply the embodiment of the unique and individual spirit of capitalism, which is not very different from the view of Parsons or Weber. It is the empirical, scientific and entirely non-metaphysical theory of man's developing technology and the accompanying forms of social organisation. The theory goes to show how advancing technology calls for a correspondingly appropriate form of human relations in the economy. It sees all this as created by the intelligence and activity of man. *This* explains Durkheim's and Parsons' functional unit, whether in the Greek city state, ancient Rome, feudal Europe or modern capitalism; *and* it explains their coming into being and their obsolescence. It also explains the irrationalities of the rational economy at a late stage of its existence; and the internal stresses and strains, and class struggles of periods of transition.

It is on this basis that we can have as effective a theory of man's self-made world as we have for the ready-made world of the natural sciences. Weber devised the method he believed would give him the same kind of laws in the *social* sciences as in the natural. But his model dealt with *existing* society instead of becoming a theory of successive forms of society and of man's creative activity in constructing them. He entirely left out of account the development of society and the radical changes involved in relation to man's growing control of nature and his ever-increasing ability to satisfy his needs and enlarge them beyond mere sufficiency.

If sociology refuses to consider such a theory, a psychologist might say it was because it *refuses to know* anything contrary to someone's interests. Or is it because of sheer stupidity and innate conservatism? In any case the obstruction and frustration by the forces capitalism has brought into being have disruptive and destructive effects, including disappointed hopes, crippled lives, and unnecessary impoverishment. The money game is the most dangerous game that men in society have ever played—more mechanistic, more impersonal and relentless in its relationships, more destructive of human disregard for humanity than any other system of exploitation. When it reaches deadlock, when desperate measures are taken to keep it going, when war offers an opportunity for using to the full economic resource forced into contraction, it endangers the existence of the whole of civilisation.

If war is averted, the exigencies of the market, the refusal to go forward, create a world of anomalies and irrationalities, of cruelty and callousness, of careless luxury and ruthless struggle between competing groups and individuals. This creates what the man without a philosophy, without a theory, with no historical perspective, with no understanding of the developmental situation, can only see as "the human predicament"—and so on the basis of his immediate experience of it seeks for consolation or falls into a philosophy of despair.

Goldman[9] has shown how each phase in the descent into crisis creates its own form of negative culture, from Schopenhauer, Nietzsche and Thomas Mann to Sartre, Kafka and Beckett—all of them forms of renunciation and impotence.

The replacement of the coherent social world of the older realists by an incoherent factuality; the disappearance of any meaningful relationship between man and his social environment; the breakdown of character, the disintegration of purpose and will; the isolation and alienation of man. . . . The distortion of reality in modernist works are true reflection of a distorted reality.[10]

These writers and dramatists mirror the reality around them *too directly*. They remain within the frontiers of bourgeois experience and therefore cannot see their world whole or the possibility of going beyond the present state of affairs, but

The question is not; is all this really there? The question is simply: is this the whole of reality? It is not: has all this not to be described? the question is simply: have we to stick at this point?[11]

Our horror, our despair, is the measure of the degree to which we are made acutely aware of our need for wholeness of personality, for a meaningful existence. It should be the function of a genuine science of society not to adapt man to the Procrustes bed of a fragmented and divisive society *in extremis*, but to show him the way to fulfilment, not as some gift of the gods or happy termination of the march of history, but as the possibility, and today the urgent necessity, of his own understanding of the human situation—how it came to be, where it is now, and where he alone can take it, if his consciousness can rise from its actual confusion and paralysis to its potential range and grasp of human history and its tasks.

NOTES

1. Weber, *Politics as a Vocation*.
2. Weber, *Gesammelte Aufsätze zur Soziologie*
3. Marianne Weber, *Max Weber*; J. P. Meyer, *Max Weber and German Politics*; H. Stuart Hughes, *Consciousness and Society*.
4. A. Kolnai, *The War against the West*.
5. F. Stern, *The Politics of Cultural Despair*.
6. In *Modern Sociological Theory*, ed. Boskoff.
7. B. F. Skinner, *Beyond Freedom and Dignity*.
8. F. Hayek, *Individualism, True or False*.
9. L. Goldman, *The Human Sciences and Philosophy*.
10. Roy Pascal, 'George Lukacs: the Concept of Totality', in *George Lukacs, the Man, his Work and his Ideals*, ed. Parkinson.
11. G. Lukacs, *The Meaning of Contemporary Realism*.

Books

By far the best introduction to Max Weber is Julian Freund's *The Sociology of Max Weber* (Allen Lane, The Penguin Press, 1968). To accompany this one should have available Eldridge's *Max Weber* in 'The Making of Sociology' series (Nelson, 1971); while the exposition is brief, the value of this book is its selection from the writings of Weber representing a wide range of his work, including material which has not, so far, been easily available. A brief and otherwise difficult to come by account of Weber's life will be found in Donald MacRae's *Weber*, in Fontana Modern Masters; but the pages devoted to the exposition of his views are too compressed to be useful.

Turning to Weber's own works, a good deal is still untranslated or rather difficult to come by, and most of it somewhat obscure to the average reader. A start could be made on his *Economy and Society* in the well-translated and prefaced volume of *Essays from Max Weber* (ed. Gerth and Mills, London, 1946). After that the two basic volumes to study are *The Methodology of the Social Sciences*, in the excellent translation by Shils and Finch (Glencoe Free Press, 1949), and *The Theory of Social and Economic*

Organisation, translated by Henderson and Talcott Parsons (Hodge, 1947).

One of the most interesting and perhaps the best known of Weber's works is *The Protestant Ethic and the Spirit of Capitalism*, also translated by Talcott Parsons. But the student would be advised to read R. H. Tawney's development of the same theme in relation to Protestantism in Britain. *Religion and the Rise of Capitalism* (Pelican) is not only a fine work of scholarship but is brilliantly written and powerfully argued.

We turn now to some major expository and critical works. In German, A. von Schelting's *Max Webers Wissenschaftslehre* is the best account of his philosophy. In English, the authoritative work is Talcott Parsons' *The Structure of Social Action*, Vol. II (Free Press). This is a first-rate and indispensable exposition. Raymond Aron's *German Sociology*, with an excellent section on Weber is unfortunately not in print, but can be found in university libraries. A very exciting and disturbing book on the political perspectives of Max Weber's sociology is Mommsen's *The Age of Bureaucracy* (Blackwell, 1974). A number of other German scholars, all of them distinguished, and some who knew and worked with Weber in Heidelberg, read papers at the Heidelberg Congress in 1964 to commemorate the centenary of Weber's birth. These papers have been edited by Otto Stammer, along with other papers by sociologists from France and the United States, including Aron and Marcuse: *Max Weber and Sociology Today* (ed. Stammer, Blackwell, 1971).

Finally, three books of a critical nature but of great importance. Lucien Goldmann, whose recent death has inflicted a grave loss, has written a critical survey of *The Human Sciences and Philosophy*, which is concerned with the tradition of Weber as it has penetrated contemporary sociology. Professor Stuart Hughes of Harvard has written an excellent book on the whole period of Weber, Pareto and the Neo-Idealist and Existentialist philosophers: *Consciousness and Society* is published in Paladin paperbacks. And then, while not specifically dealing with Weber, but covering the widest sphere of sociology in the perspective of contemporary philosophy, is Professor Ernest Gellner's *Thought and Change*, from which I have gathered many useful insights and pungent criticism, notably of the value-free theories of contemporary sociology.

A general view of the development of sociology from Durkheim to Weber is Professor Nisbet's *The Sociological Tradition* (Heinemann). This is extremely informative and of absorbing interest, and is quite the best general introduction of a constructively critical nature available to students.

Authors Quoted or Mentioned

Aron, Raymond, French sociologist, *German Sociology* (1957), *Main Currents in Sociological Thought* (1968).

Avineri, Shlomo, *The Social and Political Thought of Karl Marx* (1968).

Bell, Daniel. *The End of Ideology* (1961).

Bellamy, Edward. *Looking Backward* (1905).

Bentham, Jeremy. English political theorist.

Böhm-Bawerk, E. von. *Karl Marx and the Close of his System* (1898). Austrian economist: author of the first academic criticism of Marx's economic theory, to which Hilferding replied.

Cannon, W. *The Wisdom of the Body* (1932), the classical exposition of biological homeostasis—the self-regulating mechanisms of the body.

Collingwood, R. G. (1891–1943). *The Idea of Nature* (1945), *The Idea of History* (1946). Among his other works, notably *An Essay in Metaphysics*, and *Autobiography*. Oxford philosopher and archaeologist.

Crick, Francis. Nobel Prize winner. Discoverer with J. D. Watson of the structure of the DNA molecule.

Dahrendorf, R. *Class Conflict in an Industrial Society* (1959). Now Director of the London School of Economics.

Darwin, Charles. English scientist.

Dilthey, Wilhelm (1833–1911). *Das Erlebnis und die Dichtung* (1905), and many other works. Founder of the *Lebens-philosophie*, the philosophy of life.

Durkheim, Emile (1858–1917). *The Rules of Sociological Method* (1912), *Elementary Forms of Religious Life* (1912). French sociologist and anthropologist.

Eldridge, J. E. T. *Max Weber*, in Nelson's 'The Making of Sociology' series.

Einstein, Albert. German scientist.

Engels, F. Collabrator with Karl Marx.

Gellner, Ernest. English philosopher.

Hannington, Wal. *The Problem of the Distressed Areas*, etc. Leader of the unemployed during the depressions of the twenties and thirties.

Hayek, F. A. Formerly Professor of Economic Science in the University of London.

Hegel, G. W. F. German philosopher.

Hilferding, R. (1876–1941). *Das Finanzkapital* (1910). Economist of the Austro-Marxist school. Replied to Bohm-Bawerk's criticism of Marx.

Hobson, J. A. British economist. His *Imperialism* (1902) was recognised by Lenin as a contribution to the theory of economic imperialism which he was systematising.

Huxley, T. H. English scientist.

Jaspers, Karl (1883–   ). Existentialist German philosopher, laying emphasis on psychology and history.

Jellinek, F. *The Civil War in Spain* (1938), *The Paris Commune of 1871* (1937). German historian and friend of Max Weber.

Jünger, Ernst. Leading German philosopher of the Nazi period.

Kautsky, Karl. *The Economic Doctrines of Karl Marx* (1887). German historian and theoretician of the German Social Democratic Party. Editor of *Neue Zeit*.

Kant, Immanuel. German philosopher.

Klages, Ludwig. Ideologist of the Nazi movement. His philosophy expressed a vitalistic and instinctive spirit in the manner of Nietzsche.

Kolnai, Aurel. *The War against the West* (1938). Hungarian philosopher. His book gives a full and documented account of the ideological trends in Germany leading up to and including the culmination in the explicit ideology of the Nazi movement.

König, R. Professor of Sociology in the Universities of Cologne and Zurich.

Korsch, Karl (1886–1961). *Marxism and Philosophy* (1923). German Marxist philosopher.

Kuhn, Thomas. *The Structure of Scientific Revolutions* (1962).

Lagarde, Paul de (1827–1891). Percursor of the Germanic ideology of the Nazi movement.

Lenin, V. I. Russian communist leader.

Lipset, S. M. English sociologist.

Locke, John (1632–1704). English philosopher.

Luxemburg, Rosa (1871–1919). *The Accumulation of Capital* (1923), *Against Revisionism* (1925), *Reform and Revolution* (1899). Polish economist and revolutionary communist, Associated with the German Social Democratic Party and later with the Spartacists. Murdered in 1919.

Lukacs, Georg (1885–1971). *History and Class Consciousness* (1924), and many other works. Hungarian philosopher and literary critic.

MacRae, D. G. *Weber* (1974), in Fontana Modern Masters.

Malinowski, B. British anthropologist.

Marx, Karl. German philosopher, historian and sociologist: founder of Marxism.

Mehring, Franz (1846–1919). *Karl Marx, the Story of his Life* (English edition, 1936). German Social Democratic leader and theorist. Philosopher and literary critic.

Marcuse, Herbert (1898–). Member of the Frankfurt Institute for Social Research, which moved to the United States during the war years and has now returned to Frankfurt. Now Professor of Political Thought in the University of California. His principal works are *Reason and Revolution* (1941), *One Dimensional Man* (1964).

Mill, James. English political economist.

Möller van der Bruck, Arthur (1876–1924). *Das Dritte Reich* (1923). Leading ideologist of the Nazi movement.

Morris, William. English artist, poet and socialist.

Oakeshott, Michael. Professor of Political Science in the University of London.

Parsons, Talcott. *The Structure of Social Action* (1949). American sociologist and exponent of structural functionalism.

Plumb, J. H. *The Renaissance* (1961). *The Crisis in the Humanities* (1964). Reader in Modern History in the University of Cambridge.

Radcliffe-Brown, A. R. *Structure and Function in Primitive Society* (1925).

Ranke, Leopold von (1795–1886). German historian.

Rex, John. *Key Problems of Sociological Theory* (1961). Professor of Sociology in the University of Warwick.

Rickert, Heinrich (1863–1936). *Die Probleme der Geschichtes-philosophie* (1892). German neo-Kantian philosopher. Professor at Freiburg and Heidelberg.

Simmel, George (1858–1918). *Vom Wesen des historischen Verstehens* (1918). German philosopher and sociologist. Professor in Berlin and Strasbourg. His philosophy linked life and history in the neo-Kantian spirit.

Skinner, B. F. American behaviourist psychologist.

Smith, Adam (1723–1790). *The Wealth of Nations* (1776). English economist and moral philosopher.

Sombart, Werner (1863–1941). *Modern Capitalism* (3 volumes, 1902). Leading German sociologist and economist. Professor in the University of Berlin. Neo-Kantian of the Baden School. Formerly a Marxist, he came to believe in the peaceful evolution of capitalism into 'social pluralism'.

Spengler, Oswald (1880–1936). *The Decline of the West* (1918–1922). German historian and philosopher.

Spann, Othmar. Austrian philosopher of 'the anti-individualist universal state'. Leading German ideologist of the Nazi period.

Stuart-Hughes, H. American social philosopher, professor at Harvard.

Spencer, Herbert. English philosopher and sociologist.

Stern, Fritz (1926–   ) *The Politics of Cultural Despair* (1961). A study of the rise of the Germanic ideology. Also *Der wahre Staat* (1931).

Tocqueville, Comte de (1805–1859). *De la Démocratie en Amerique* (1835). French critic of American democracy.

Tönnies, Ferdinand (1855–1936). *Gemeinschaft und Gesellschaft* (1887). Influential German economist and sociologist. Professor in Kiel. Chairman of the German Sociological Society founded by Weber.

Toynbee, Arnold. *A Study of History* (9 volumes, 1951–1954).

Troeltsch, Ernst (1865–1923). German philosopher and theologian. Professor at Heidelberg and Berlin.

Tugan-Baranowski. *Theoretical Foundations of Marxism* (1905). Russian émigré resident in Western Europe. Marxist revisionist. Kautsky wrote a famous reply to the above book.

Walsh, David. *New Directions in Sociological Theory* (1972). British sociologist, Goldsmith's College, University of London; with colleagues Silverman and Philipson has advanced a phenomenological sociology called Ethno-methodology.

Watson, J. D. With Crick discovered the spiral helix of the DNA molecule.

Whitehead, A. N. (1861–1947). English philosopher and mathematician, resident in America since 1924 as Professor at Harvard. With Bertrand Russell wrote *Principia Mathematica*. *Process and Reality* is his major philosophical work, but *Modes of Thought* and *Science and the Modern World* have perhaps been more influential.

Wright-Mills, C. American economist and sociologist.